GOD
It's About Fellowship

by

Claudia G. Lindsey

• WRITE WAY •
PUBLISHING COMPANY
RALEIGH, NORTH CAROLINA

GOD
Copyright © 2016 by Claudia G. Lindsey

Unless otherwise indicated, all Scripture quotations are taken from the New International Version (NIV) of the Bible, copyright ©1978, 1984 by International Bible Society. Used by permission of Zondervan Publishing House. All rights reserved.

All rights reserved under International Copyright Law. Contents and or cover may not be reproduced in whole or in part without the express written consent of the Publisher. Contact the publisher at info@writewaypublishingcompany.com.

Printed in the United States of America.

ISBN: 978-1946425621

Formerly printed under ISBN: 13: 978-1534986930

Library of Congress: 2017953021

Book interior by CSinclaire Write-Design
Cover design and imagery: Cary A. Lindsey

First printing, 2017
Second printing, 2020

www.writewaypublishingcompany.com

Acknowledgements

Special thanks to Todd Burpo for writing *Heaven is for Real* revealing scenes in heaven as witnessed by his son. The throne room was not seen as an austere, foreboding place but a place where Christ holds a child in his lap, the Holy Spirit reveals things, and God is conceived as a "big" God.

Sincere gratitude and honor to Watchman Nee. His many talks and sermons, now compiled into several books such as *Changed into His Likeness*, helped inspire this writing.

Notes on the first five books of the Bible, written by a person who identifies himself only by C.H.M., were inspirational references.

Heartfelt appreciation and love is extended to my sister, Barbara, and my son, Arden, for their encouragement, support and helpful suggestions.

Much gratitude and thanks to Dr. Kevin Snyder, Lee Heinrich, and Charlotte Sinclaire without whose favor, expertise, and help this book would not have been published

C.G.L.

To My Posterity

"Even when I am old and gray
Do not forsake me, O God,
Till I declare your power to the
next generation,
Your might to all who are to come."

Psalm 71:18

"Walk about Zion, go around her,
count her towers,
consider well her ramparts,
view her citadels,
that you may tell of them
to the next generation.
For this God is our God for ever and ever;
He will be our guide even to the end."

Psalm 48:12-14

Table of Contents

Preface   ix

One — Thoughts of God   1

Two — Know the God of Abraham   8

Three — Know the God of Isaac   16

Four — Know the God of Jacob   24

Five — Christ the Sacrifice   36

Six — Divine Love   48

Seven — It's About Fellowship   56

Preface

∼

"You are searching for God, the idea of God in his essential being. You seek perfection and it lies in everything that happens to you—your suffering, your actions, your impulses are the mysteries under which God reveals himself to you. But he will never disclose himself in the shape of that exalted image to which you so vainly cling."

Jean Pierre De Caussade

There is no presumption in entitling this writing *GOD* for it has to do with a quest for God and a desire to know Him. There are no new truths, and revelation is a known truth, which becomes real in a person's life when head knowledge becomes heart knowledge. Much of this work is derived from a serious study of the Pentateuch. Truths gleaned from books, sermons, people, and experiences—from scripture, meditation, and revelation—have settled within and asked expression. It is hoped that reading this book will create an urgent longing to know and fellowship with God who is gracious, righteous, compassionate, and sovereign.

GOD

1

Thoughts of God

> "Be still and know that I am God;
> I will be exalted in the earth."
>
> Psalm 46:10

God! Magnificent! Majestic! Infinite! Can finite man know this seemingly unapproachable God? May he know Him? Are there any whose heart-cry is, "I want to know Him"? "My goal is God himself, at any cost, dear Lord, by any road."[1]

There is none but God—all else is His creation. God created earth to be inhabited, and He created people for Himself. "Know that the Lord is God. It is he who made us and we are his; we are his people, the sheep of his pasture" (Psalm 100:3). God, who forms the hearts of all, leaves an empty space therein that only He is able to fill. There is a longing within, a reaching for something more, for something other. Nothing created, nothing finite can allay this haunting need. No parent, spouse, or child, no endeavor or success, no pleasure, no amount of money will assuage this inner emptiness, this restless searching for God. "In the night my soul yearns for you; in the morning my spirit

---
[1] Oswald Chambers, *My Utmost for His Highest*, November 17 devotion.

longs for you" (Isaiah 26:9). God put this need for Himself into the hearts of people because of His want of them. He created mankind to satisfy His holy passion for a people with whom He could fellowship, a worshipping people upon whom He could lavish His boundless love—a people to love Him. Divine desire for such a people sent Jesus to the cross. It's about fellowship.

God introduces Himself as the everlasting God and as the only God. "I am the first and the last. Apart from me there is no God" (Isaiah 4:6). Scripture reveals the Trinity as Father, Son, and Holy Spirit but also proclaims that God is one and speaks of His fullness. God in His fullness and oneness affirms the truth of the inseparable Trinity. The Triune God communicates a unity that envelopes and transcends everything and from whom all things flow. Unity expresses the unvaried and uniform character of the Three in One.

The Oneness of God

There is one Godhead. Within the Godhead, there are no separate agendas, opposing ideas, diverse plans, or power struggles. "Christ, who being in very nature God, did not consider equality with God something to be grasped" (Philippians 2:6). Oneness of thought and mind is apparent in the purpose of God, the Word of God, and the love of God. Jesus said, "I and the Father are one" (John 10:30). The Holy Spirit is spoken of as the Spirit of Christ and the Spirit of God.

A simple illustration of the oneness of the Trinity often used and easily understood is water in its different forms. Water flows like a river, freezes like an iceberg, and becomes steam over a boiling cauldron. Scripture does not proclaim there is one God but rather that God is one. "Hear, O Israel: The Lord our God, the Lord is one" (Deuteronomy 6:4). Lord, in the Hebrew, is here used in a plural form. Paraphrased, this might read that the plurality of God is one. A paradox in any language, it engrosses the mind with wonder.

Another example of Divine oneness is man himself. Created in the image of God, he is body, soul, and spirit. The physical being is not the image of God; the soul—the person, the personality—is not the image of God, nor is the spirit of man. It is spirit, soul, and body in one that is meant by created in His image. This gives some understanding of the oneness of God. Man is one, yet he is tripartite; he can live according to his spirit, his soul, or his flesh. When he dies, the spirit returns to God who gave it and the body to the earth from which it came. The soul will appear before Christ to hear an eternal pronouncement.

God is the transcendent Father and the immanent Holy Spirit. He is the incarnate Son who came to earth with flesh and blood. How profound is the oneness of the Triune God.

The Fullness of God

Jesus reveals God in His fullness, for it pleased God to have all His fullness dwell in Him. Christ, the Mighty God, will be called Wonderful Counselor, Everlasting Father, Prince of Peace—the fullness of God. The immanent Holy Spirit and the transcendent Father became incarnate in the Son. Jesus Christ articulates to humanity that which otherwise cannot be defined or expressed. "The people walking in darkness have seen a great light; on those living in the land of the shadow of death a light has dawned" (Isaiah 9:2).

A person can know and experience God, but human powers cannot comprehend His infinite depths and breadth or His understanding. God Almighty is omniscient, omnipotent, and omnipresent. He is all-seeing and all-hearing. God, having life in Himself, is omnificent, life-germinating, and life-sustaining.

The fullness of God embodies all truth, beauty, and goodness. In man's search for these quintessential riches, all roads lead to God.

Truth is treasure. God is truth. His word is truth, and His word declares it is impossible for God to lie. The word of the Lord is flawless and declares what is right. God's written word or spoken word is always trustworthy. Contemplating a course of action, I heard, "Do not do this, it is not the King's way; my blessing will not be on this." The God of truth had spoken.

Evidence of the truth is everywhere. Creation testifies to the truth. How can an intelligent person, why would anyone—seeing the beauty and ecology of nature with all its complexities, the design and creation of earth, galaxies, the universe, the immensities of space and its sustainability—deny a divine and infinite intelligence. No earthling can even build a doghouse without a plan, the materials, and the ability to carry it out. Yet fools think that creation—earth and space beyond man's ability to comprehend or mathematically calculate—exploded into existence, fell into place, and everything remains on course. There is the minuteness and power of the atom to contemplate. Could not one with wide-eyed wonder ask what formed the first matter and how gravity came to be?

Creation, the universe, many universes defy the understanding of the most brilliant and learned of men. Therefore, it is incumbent upon mankind to acknowledge the truth. An infinite being of divine nature and eternal power created the heavens and the earth and set them in motion.

Lift your eyes to the heavens and see a grand display of divine intelligence. The skies proclaim His handiwork—their voice is heard at sunrise and sunset, in the sunshine, in the clouds, and in the storm. At night, they display knowledge. Scripture declares that God's command formed the universe and that He made what is seen from what was not seen. When He spoke, it came to be, and when He commanded, it stood firm. Can any astronomical genius offer a more credible, conceivable, or provable explanation?

Foreknowledge, fulfilled prophecy, and profound wisdom for living as found in scripture attest to the truth. Changed lives and answered prayers testify to the truth. History and the Bible agree. There are no discrepancies between true science and the Bible. Yet knowledge of the truth escapes many. Christ, having been falsely accused, was brought before Pilot, the governor of Judea. Arrogant and befuddled, Pilot asked, "What is truth?" Truth was standing before him.

Beauty and holiness are synonymous. Perfection is beautiful, holiness is perfection, and God is holy. "My mouth is filled with your praise, declaring your splendor all day long" (Psalm 71:8).

Before going into battle, King Jehoshaphat of ancient Judah appointed singers to go ahead of the army and sing praise to the Lord for the beauty of His holiness. King David prayed that he might dwell in the house of the Lord all the days of his life to behold the beauty of the Lord. The Lord Almighty is holy. "Your eyes will see the King in his beauty" (Isaiah 33:17a).

Goodness is love in action. God is good. What He does is good. He is good all the time. The Psalms proclaim: Good and upright is the Lord…Taste and see that the Lord is good…Celebrate His abundant goodness.

A relative, betrayed and deserted, trusted in the goodness of God; later she found herself still standing and whole, looking at bright skies. A story, read long ago, told of a man who continued to praise God for His goodness though "all he claimed was swept away. His ambitions, plans, and wishes, at his feet in ashes lay."[2] God restored and increased his fortune. Naomi, of the Bible, after the death of her husband and both sons said, "I went away full, but the Lord has brought me back empty" (Ruth 1:21). Then she rejoiced in the goodness of God when later, elate with life, she held a grandbaby in her arms.

Though the heart is sick with sorrow if a loved one does not get well or when fortunes are not restored—give thanks to the Lord for He is good. His love never fails. Doubt, anger, fretting, and self-pity produce hopelessness, and the glory and goodness of God are obscured. If a person ceases to seek and trust the Lord, he denies himself the strength and comfort of a good and sustaining God. Wait for the Lord. He works for the good of those who love Him, and His faithfulness endures forever. "Taste and see that the Lord is good; blessed are all who take refuge in Him" (Psalm 34:8).

The Trinity of God

The Trinity reveals the greatness, the nearness, and the Word of God. God, high and lofty who lives forever, whose name is holy,

---
[2] J. M. Harris, "I will Praise Him" song lyrics

and who lives in a high and holy place, conveys the transcendence and greatness of the Father. The nearness of God is made known by the immanent Holy Spirit, for He lives with those who are contrite and lowly in spirit—the human being visited by the divine. In Jesus, the incarnate Son, humanity and the divine came together—the intangible becoming tangible. "The Word became flesh and made His dwelling among us. We have seen his glory, the glory of the One and Only who came from his Father, full of grace and truth" (John 1:14).

Genesis chapter one immediately introduces the Trinity. God the Father is the beginning and source of everything as "In the beginning God…" shows. God as Spirit is present when the "Spirit of God was hovering over the water…." "And God said…" reveals Jesus, the Word, who was with God in the beginning. "Through Him all things were made; nothing that has been made was made without him" (John 1:3).

A triune God is revealed by the office and function of each. The Father plans, the Son speaks, the Holy Spirit does. God the Father chooses and calls, Jesus is Lord and Savior, the Holy Spirit sanctifies. The transcendent Father is the Majesty in heaven, the incarnate Son is King over all creation, and the immanent Holy Spirit is the power. As Father, God is the lawgiver, God the Son is the judge, God the Holy Spirit is executor. This is the government of God. Scripture discloses the mind, emotions, and will of the Father—the soul of God, if you will. Jesus, displaying His sinless perfection and unblemished righteousness, is God in the flesh. God the Holy Spirit is the Presence—the finite experiencing the infinite.

God is everlasting. His understanding no one can fathom. His judgments are unsearchable; His ways past finding out. Who has known the mind of the Lord or been His counselor? Yet, what may be known about God has been made plain by what He has created. Not only so, but God has revealed Himself and made known His purpose in the lives and experiences of Abraham, Isaac, and Jacob. His name and character are involved with them.

Trinitarian truths are clearly seen in the lives of these three men, for God identifies Himself as the God of Abraham, the God of Isaac, and the God of Jacob. Linked together many times in scripture, they represent the Trinity, not in their humanness, but by their place in history and God's design.

Each man exemplifies a unique experience of God. Abraham knew God the Father, the source of everything. Isaac knew God as the Giver and the all-sufficient Gift. Jacob knew the ever-present Holy Spirit, the God of all comfort who leads and guides, who teaches and trains. Their pilgrimage is the Christian's pilgrimage set forth in vivid relief. The combined experiences of these three men will be the spiritual experience of all who desire to know God.

GOD

2

Know the God of Abraham

"The Lord is my strength and my shield, my heart trusts in him and I am helped."

Psalm 28:7

Abraham's life points to God the Father, and he typifies Him because so many things began with him. God's plan of redemption began with Abraham, for he was the first called out one. He was the first Hebrew. God is known as Father, and Abraham is a father figure. The father of many nations, Abraham is also the father of all who believe and the father of the faithful. Like God, he was a father willing to sacrifice his one and only son.

God chose Abraham, first known as Abram, and called him out of a world of darkness and into His kingdom of light. Identify with Abram. He is a sinner and an idolater, but God called him. He is to turn his back on the world and be a stranger on earth, a pilgrim passing through. God will be his God and God will be his Father. When his sojourn on Earth is ended, he is promised eternal life in a heavenly country.

The Call

Captivated and awed by the presence of the God of Glory, Abram answers His call. Awakened to new beginnings, at God's behest, Abram leaves his country and his countrymen to go to a place God will show him. Abram, his brother and their father, a nephew and their wives leave Ur of the Chaldeans in response to God's call to Abram. Abram has been singled out for a special purpose, but none are turned away who respond to God. Abram is often criticized for incomplete obedience for bringing family with him and for delayed obedience because he settled in Haran. Recorded scripture does not support this. It seems clear that God had not yet shown him where he was to go. "He obeyed and went, even though he did not know where he was going" (Hebrews 11:8). The call was to leave country, countrymen, and kinsmen—not family. God, in His wisdom, did not send Abram on a lone journey. It is apparent that God planned to have people in Haran who were related to Abram, a people familiar with and influenced by Abram's God.

While living in Haran, Abram again hears God's call, "leave this country and your father's people and go now to the land I will show you" (Genesis 12:1). Abram left Haran with his beautiful wife Sarai, and maybe he could take his nephew Lot.

Abram, arriving in Canaan, is in the land to which God has called him. God would make him into a great nation, he would be blest, his name would be great, and all peoples on earth would be blest through him. This chosen land is where God's writ would be established and His purpose fulfilled.

Altars

The place names of the three altars Abram built in Canaan have spiritual significance. He traveled to Shechem and came to the great tree of Moreh. "The Lord appeared to Abram and said, 'To your offspring I will give this land.' So he built an altar there to the Lord who had appeared to him" (Genesis 12:7). The word Shechem refers to strength. Abram's faith of obedience brought him to the land of God's choosing—this is the place of strength. "Blessed are those whose strength is in you, who have set their hearts on pilgrimage" (Psalm 84:5). Moreh relates to teacher or teaching and implies learning and understanding. Strength for living comes from God, and learning to rely on Him is crucial. Pulsating throughout all of Abram's experiences is an underlying theme—God is the source; rely on Him.

Bethel translates to "House of God," a place of worship. Abram built a second altar here and called on the name of the Lord. He traveled on toward the Negev, but a severe famine caused him to go to Egypt. Abram is no longer in the land of God's choosing. There are no altars in Egypt. In this weakened position, he fails to rely on God for protection and commits sin.

Abram departed Egypt but found no resting place until he returned to the place he had last called on the name of the Lord—a conspicuous spiritual truth. "From the Negev he went from place to place until he came to Bethel and Ai where his tent had been earlier and where he had built an altar. There Abram called on the name of the Lord" (Genesis 13:3-4). God called Abram to the land of Canaan. Whenever he left this chosen land, he found himself in disrepute.

Abram's sojourn into Egypt foreshows the Israelites who also went there because of a famine. Egypt represents the bondage of sin. While there, Abram sinned. The Israelites were in bondage. Abram left Egypt with great wealth, as did the Israelites, an augury of the wealth received in Christ when freed from sin's bondage. Abram wandered until he returned to Bethel, the place of worship. The Israelites wandered in the desert and found no rest until they were in the Promised Land. If a believer strays from the chosen path, he finds no peace until he returns to the place of blessing.

Before building a third altar in Hebron, Abram realizes Lot has to be dealt with. God's call is to Abram. He will give this land to him and his descendants and make of him a great nation. Lot is not included in God's purpose for Abram. Lot and his herdsmen have become a problem, so Abram separates from him. Lot settles in the fertile valley of the plains south of Canaan and pitches his tent toward the city of Sodom.

Abram came to Hebron and pitched his tent near the great trees of Mamre. Hebron, by definition, means in association with or fellowship. Here Abram makes three friends and allies. More importantly, he is in fellowship with God, for here he builds another altar. Mamre speaks of vigor. Later, Abram is seen in vigorous and personal fellowship with God. God confides His intentions for Sodom and Gomorrah, and Abram boldly intercedes for the doomed city of Sodom. He prays about being childless, and God promises him a son, and he is again promised the land. In fellowship with God, he offers the sacrifices of God's choosing but has to drive away the birds of prey—a rich spiritual truth. Doubt, dismay, and despair are despoilers and can sabotage a commitment. God reveals to Abram what will happen to his descendants to the fourth generation. All this happened in Hebron, the place of fellowship.

Tests

Abram answered God's call. He has trusted and obeyed his Father God. In accordance with His will, he is living in the land of God's choosing and has built altars to Him. Why then must he be tested? Tests and trials come so that faith and commitment may be proven genuine. God tests a person for "when he has tested me, I will come forth as gold" (Job 23:10). Gold, a symbol of God, has to do with godliness. Abram's first test concerns the world. "If anyone loves the world, the love of the Father is not in him" (1 John 2:15b). Does Abram's heart belong to God?

Sitting in front of his tent in peace and comfort, secure in the promises of God, Abram is alerted to the horror of the now. War had broken out in the southern plains. Five kings from there had been defeated. The victors had captured the people and Lot and his family are prisoners. Lot may have been spiritually weak but Abram had to help his "brother." Abram took his trained servants, and, with his three friends, raided the camp that held the captives. He recovered the people and the spoils of Sodom.

Abram, weary and tired from the battle, is met by Melchizedek, the priest of God Most High. King of righteousness and peace,

Melchizedek refreshes Abram with bread and wine and blesses him saying, "Blessed be Abram by God Most High, creator of heaven and earth. And blessed be God Most High, who has delivered your enemies into your hand. Then Abram gave him a tenth of everything" (Genesis 14:19-20).

Sodom's king also met with Abram. He wanted him to return the people and offered him the spoils of Sodom as a reward. This is the test! Will Abram take all this wealth and be beholden to an ungodly King? Abram determined that the king of Sodom could never say he had made Abram rich. Besides the moral and spiritual defeat Abram would have suffered by accepting the Sodomite's offer, he might have put himself in grave danger should the king want to reclaim his treasures. "It is better to take refuge in the Lord than to trust in princes" (Psalm118:9). Abram knew God as the source of his blessing, victory, and protection—and God Himself, his very great reward. His heart belonged to God.

If tempted to sin or do something in opposition to God's will, to hold onto something God has forbidden or asked for, look within and gain understanding. Is the heart divided? "…give me an undivided heart that I may fear your name" (Psalm 86: 11b).

Abram's second test was a test of waiting, waiting, waiting—waiting for God's time. Promised a son and offspring as countless as the stars, he believed God, but he is old and Sarai is barren; she offers Abram her slave Hagar to have his child. Abram did not doubt God, but he could do this; he could help God fulfill His promise. Hagar bore Abram a son. What he got for his effort was Ishmael, a wild donkey of a man. His hand would be against everyone and everyone's hand would be against him; he would live in hostility to all his brothers.

Tangled circumstances result. Sarai and Hagar are at enmity. As a boy, Ismael is a troublemaker and though Abram loves him, he sends him away—rejected from being a patriarch of Israel and disqualified for fulfilling God's purpose. Long-term consequences result. Ishmael's descendants have always hated and been a threat to Israel.

God appears to Abram again when he is ninety-nine years old and at once makes known His holy standard. To affirm His holy standard, God changes Abram's name to Abraham and Sarai's to Sarah. Adding the "h" identified them with Jehovah, a holy God. "Christian" identifies a person with Christ.

To confirm His demand for holiness, God institutes the covenant of circumcision. God has said, "But just as he who called you is holy, so be holy in all you do" (1 Peter 1:15). Relevant to today, a circumcision of the heart—a divine wound—teaches a person to rely on God and to put no confidence in corrupted flesh.

Abraham is again promised a son. At ninety-nine, Abraham's strength is gone. As good as dead, he has to rely on God for the promised son. God does His mighty work when the flesh is given over to death. When faced with a decision, it helps to remember what was learned at the altar and to live up to what has already been attained. "Be still before the Lord and wait patiently for Him…" (Psalm 37:7a). God heals Sarah and enables Abraham to become a father. Isaac, the one through whom Abraham's seed will be reckoned, is born.

Abraham's third test has to do with sacrifice. God said, "Take your son Isaac, whom you love, and go to the region of Moriah. Sacrifice him there as a burnt offering…" (Genesis 22:2). Isaac is the son of promise, God's gift. It is through Isaac that God's covenant will be established, an everlasting covenant for his descendants. Does Abraham love the gift more than the Giver? Is his hope in the covenant and the treasured gift or in God?

Ministry, a spiritual experience, or a personal ambition that takes pre-eminence at the neglect of God produces leanness of soul. Grasping a gift of God, a talent, or an assignment as a personal possession renders a person ineffective in the work of the Kingdom, and then one often becomes a hindrance. Hold everything with an open hand. All can be done without save God alone. If He asks for something, relinquish it. Release it without bitterness. "By faith Abraham, when God tested him, offered Isaac as a sacrifice. He who had received the promises was about to sacrifice his one and only son, even though God had said to him, 'It is through Isaac that your offspring will be reckoned.' Abraham reasoned that God could raise the dead, and figuratively speaking, he did receive Isaac back from death" (Hebrews 11:17-19).

In a relationship with God, there is a place of abandonment reached for but illusive to the grasp. Abraham had arrived at such a place when God told him to sacrifice his son. All his fresh springs are in God, and it is with God he has to do. He can with confidence say, "I and the boy go over there, we will worship and then we will come back to you" (Genesis 22:5). Abraham, his faith being made complete, has reached that coveted place where there is none but God.

The Journey

Abraham relied on God as his source and strength but was active and involved with his responsibilities. In obedience, Abraham had made two long journeys. He was in charge of increasing and caring for his flocks and herds. Abraham built altars. Doing rightly, he rescued Lot and paid tithes to Melchizedek. God's covenant of circumcision was quickly obeyed. He interceded for Sodom. In Hebron, he sacrificed and then protected what he had offered. A man of faith, he responded to God's will and went to Mt. Moriah to sacrifice. Abraham, who trusted, obeyed, and relied on God, was productive and involved with life. Failure and frustration accompany neglecting to do, or expecting God to do, that which one is responsible for or assuming the burden of trying to do what only God can do.

Abraham's encounters with God—the answered call, the altars he built, and tests he faced—brought him into a close relationship with God. Journey with Abraham for his sojourn is every believer's sojourn. Rescued from the dominion of darkness and brought into the kingdom of light, the people of God are pilgrims and strangers on Earth. The Eternal City beckons. Abraham knew God as Father, and "How great is the love the Father has lavished upon us, that we should be called the children of God, and that is what we are" (1 John 3:1). God, "Abba Father," is trustworthy; it is safe to obey, confide in, and rely on Him. Altars are built to know, worship, and fellowship with God. His children are tested and tried to prove their faith genuine and their hearts undivided. As with Abraham, when set upon by devious, tangled, or profound circumstances, God is present to give new strength, new hope, and new life.

Abraham knew the God of Glory, the source of life and strength. He knew the transcendent Father whose standard is holiness. God most high, as Abraham knew Him, seems unapproachable and His standard of holiness unobtainable.

But God has made provision—know God as Isaac knew Him…

GOD

3

Know the God of Isaac

"...how much more will those who receive
God's abundant provision of grace
and of the gift of righteousness
reign in life through the
one man Jesus."

Romans 5:17

Isaac's life points to the Son of God. More than any other, his life typifies the life of Jesus. Like Jesus, his conception was a miracle and his birth the result of a promise. Ishmael, born in the ordinary way, persecuted the son born by the power of the Spirit. Jesus, the promised Messiah conceived by the Spirit and born of a virgin, is persecuted by people of the earth. Isaac, like Christ Jesus, was referred to as the one and only son and offered as a sacrifice. Christ rose from the dead, and figuratively speaking, Isaac was received back from death.

Isaac did what his father had done before him. Like his father, he was a nomad who kept flocks and herds, dug wells, and increased wealth. He too had to bless his second son. Jesus said, "I tell you the truth, the Son can do nothing by himself, he can do only what he sees the

Father doing, because whatever the Father does the Son also does" (John 5:19).

Abraham, Isaac's father, chose who his son's bride should be and sent an envoy, a type of the Holy Spirit, to claim her. His agent gave her jewels, indicative of the work of the Spirit, and he brought her from a far country, but she was family. God the Father chooses the bride of Christ and the Holy Spirit puts His seal upon her. She is from the earth, but she is family. "Both the one who makes men holy and those who are made holy are of the same family" (Hebrews 2:11).

Isaac planted a field in a foreign land and reaped a hundredfold harvest. Christ likened himself to a grain of wheat, which falls to the ground and dies producing many seeds. By His death on earth, the man from heaven is reaping a manifold harvest, bringing many to glory. Isaac was Abraham's sole heir. God appointed Christ heir of all things.

The Heir and the Christian

All Isaac needed was supplied by a loving father; he was born into wealth and never knew lack. Isaac knew God as the giver, typified by his father, Abraham, who provided for him and whose wealth he inherited. Isaac, the receiver, illustrates and foretells the riches a child of God receives when he is born into the Kingdom of Heaven. Everyone who receives Jesus Christ as Savior is a child of God and is born into wealth. The plentiful supply and the abundant life is Jesus. Receiving Him, there is no lack. The wealth is a spiritual inheritance to make a believer's life full and complete and to equip one to live without fault in a crooked and wicked world.

The role of a Christian is to receive; he has nothing in himself, nothing that he has not received. Christ Jesus, God's gift, is the believer's redemption, righteousness, wisdom, and holiness. These are not separate gifts; there is one gift, it is Christ Jesus. God so loved that He gave His one and only Son.

The gift is sufficient. The problem most persons have is in receiving; they receive Christ as their Savior, but fail to receive Him as their life.

People ask God for things—for health, money, patience, self-control, or whatever the present need or want may be. Riches, spiritual or financial, do not result. It is a longing for Jesus, a desire to know Him, and an ongoing enjoyment of Him that satisfies the heart and enriches the life. "My heart says of you 'Seek his face! Your face, Lord, I will seek'" (Psalm 27:8). It's about fellowship.

In Christ

The incomparable riches of God's grace have put the believer in Christ Jesus. This is not a favor to pray for nor is it something a person strives for or spiritually grows into. It is a statement of the believer's standing before God. In Christ, a child of God is accepted as one who has died with Him, been raised with Him, and ascended with Him. Seated with Christ in heavenly places, God the Father sees His child in Christ.

In Christ, past sins have been dealt with by the blood of Jesus. The repentant sinner has been cleansed, forgiven, and redeemed through the precious blood of Jesus. Something more is needed, for man is a sinner by birth. In Christ, the "old self" inherited from Adam was crucified with Him. Dying with Christ has dealt with the sinner. The soul did not die, man is not dead in himself, his flesh did not die, sin and Satan did not die. If a person still has trouble with the sin that so easily entangles, he has forgotten that he has been cleansed from his past sins and has failed to ascertain he is in Christ. "No one who lives in him keeps on sinning" (1 John 3:6a).

Those born of God are in Christ; spiritual life depends on believing, receiving, and living by this knowledge. See one's self in Christ and remain there by faith. In Christ is a wondrous, safe, and glorious place to be. The need is to search diligently to know the many ways one is united with Him. Believers are united with him not only in death but in resurrection and ascension. Christ's victories and triumphs, in flowing supply, are riches which God's grace has made available to those in Christ Jesus. Though having no righteousness, rights, title, or privileges in themselves, believers have all in Him. How unsearchable are the riches of Christ!

Christ Within

Those who have died with Christ have been raised with Him to new life. Born again, they have the Spirit of Christ living within, and the Christian life is lived when a person lives by His life. Paul, the apostle, wrote, "I no longer live but Christ lives in me" (Galatians 2:20). Christ within is sufficient for the present and the future, for the redeemed possess His life. Filled with His joy, they enjoy His peace and radiate His glory. Jesus Christ is holy, righteous, patient, kind, forgiving, and good. His attitude is always right. Live by the Spirit of the indwelling Christ that the perfections of His life may be revealed. "We who are alive are always being given over to death for Jesus sake, so that his life may be revealed in our mortal body" (2 Corinthians 4:11).

Denying the self-life does not infer doing or being nothing. God created mankind with personality and functionality. Endowed with intelligence, abilities, and talents, this self should not be neglected or denied. To train, perfect, and use these God-given capabilities is as it should be. Life is good; there is beauty to enrich, pleasures to enjoy, goals to set, work to do, roads to travel, and dreams to fulfill. "In all your ways acknowledge him and he will make your paths straight" (Proverbs 3:6).

Everyone has an innate desire for self-fulfillment. Genuine self-fulfillment is realized when life is lived for the glory of God. If a performance, a project, or a job in the work-a-day world is done as unto the Lord, work becomes noble, life's burdens lighter, and all endeavors worthwhile. Whatever abilities, talents, or accomplishments are to one's credit, may he, like Paul, consider them as nothing compared to the surpassing greatness of knowing Christ. The self that needs to die daily is the self that overrides the life and beauty of Jesus, the self who wants to live independent of God and who seeks after worthless things.

Dying with Christ frees the believer from sin's bondage. "For we know that our old self was crucified with him so that the body of sin might be done away with…because anyone who has died has been freed from sin" (Romans 6:6). This should not be confused with dying to self that Christ may be revealed. "If anyone would come after me he must deny himself and take up his cross daily and follow me. For whoever wants to save his life will lose it, but whoever loses his life for my sake will find it" (Luke 9:23-24).

If a person fails to deny his self-life, as the scripture teaches, he will not rely on Christ to be his life. Is one willing to give up his animosities and prejudices, his fears and doubts, his angers, and his right to himself that the treasure within may be seen and not the earthen vessel? Because good intentions are often misdirected and mistimed, even the self that wants to do good gets in the way. "This is how God showed his love among us, he sent his one and only son into the world that we might live through him" (1 John 4:9). This is a work in progress, and the pressing need is total surrender to Him.

Truth, beauty, and goodness are in abundant supply if indeed the Spirit of Christ dwells in the heart. Would that the truth, beauty, and goodness of Jesus be seen rather than the ugliness that so often besets self. Silver in the wilderness tabernacle symbolized Christ and redemption. Silver is refined by repeated liquidizing. Impurities float to the top and are removed. It is pure when the silversmith looks and sees nothing but his own reflection. When Jesus looks at those He has redeemed, He desires to see a reflection of Himself. Would that family, friends, loved ones, outsiders, and lost ones see Jesus when they encounter one who calls himself "Christian."

To take up one's cross, this daily dying and denying the self-life, does not mean that one is inert, insensate, characterless, or without personality. Denying the self-life has to do with letting the Spirit of Christ within react to life and its challenges through one's person instead of the self which may be unfair, unkind, biased, and out of order. This is not an effort; the Spirit within lives and operates when self is denied. Many know *about* Jesus Christ, but to *know* Him is to become like Him in His death so that one might experience the power of His resurrection—the new life within.

The Inheritance

Isaac knew God as the Giver, typified by Abraham his father. More expressly, he knew God as the gift, noted by the wealth he inherited—a symbol of Christ. Isaac's riches were real and tangible, but the inheritance could only benefit him if he lived on the abundance of what he had received. It would be hard to imagine Isaac saying, "I have no need of the inheritance. I'd rather make it on my own." Would he have been content to live on meager earnings when all this wealth was his? How does a believer possess and live on the wealth he has inherited?

Jesus Christ Himself—in Christ and Christ within—is the inheritance. This is God's doing. It is by faith a child of God receives the inheritance that enables him to live in victory and appropriate its blessings. One does not obtain his inheritance by striving; it is a gift to receive.

God has put the believer in Christ; it is by faith a person abides there. "Remain in me and I will remain in you" (John 15:4a). Christ within happens at new birth. The Trinity lives in the innermost depths of a child of God. "Do you not realize that Christ Jesus is in you—" (2 Corinthians 13:5b). "Don't you know that God's Spirit lives in you?" (1 Corinthians 3:16). "Do you not know that your body is a temple of the Holy Spirit, who is in you…?" (1 Corinthians 6:19). Gather all thoughts and energies to the innermost chamber of one's being and find God. When conscience of His presence within, all else becomes as nothing. One has found the "pearl of great price."

Jesus returned to heaven and sits at the right hand of God. Prayers are said to "our Father in heaven." The hovering Holy Spirit of God is everywhere. He lives in earthly vessels, within the spirits of persons made holy by the blood of the Lamb, and this is where His voice is heard, His wisdom imparted, and His will discerned. God makes His presence known at His good pleasure, and no self-effort will hasten or bring this joy. A person might show Him the cancer, the damaged heart, or the painful wound, but whenever God makes His presence known, there are no words. One is silenced into wondering reverence. Wordless adoration and worship flow from the heart.

Life, the inheritance, begins when a person receives Christ as Savior; life abundant, when one receives Christ as his life. The inheritance received endures, but its benefits are reaped by denying the self-life.

Isaac inherited great wealth. One must also remember that he was willing to be sacrificed—a profound and laden analogy. Any teaching that living for Christ is a life of ease and material riches is misleading. Copious blessings, fulfillment, and peace come to those living for Christ, and some are blessed with riches. The ways of the Lord are pleasant, and He has promised eternal life. Should one count the cost, it will cost everything he has; nothing is his. The way is straight and narrow, there are tests and trials, and self must be given over to death.

Would the heart stay true if one could not sense His reassuring presence, if wounded or betrayed in the house of friends or by loved ones, if persecuted by enemies? Hearts cry out for persons, for young people who will rise to the challenge. Caught in the web of God's love, experience the abundance of the inheritance, real self-fulfillment, and the sustaining joy of the Lord. Envision the eternal reward. Think of Jesus and the price he paid to save all—and the cost should one's soul be lost.

In outright love and grace, God has put the believer in Christ. Christ within is the mystery that has been hidden for ages. "God has chosen to make known the glorious riches of this mystery, which is Christ in you, the hope of glory" (Colossians 1:27). Christ within is greater than the one who is in the world. His indwelling Spirit outdistances any other power, love, or pleasure. He is the source of strength, and living by the Spirit enables one to be holy. At His right hand are pleasures forevermore. This is an extravagant inheritance.

Isaac's life foreshows the riches a child of God has inherited—the life of Christ within and the privilege to live by His life. If a person lives by the Spirit, he portrays the Word of God; God's Word is truth. He fulfills the purpose of his life, a display of the goodness of God. The life of the Spirit is an expression of God and reveals the beauty of Jesus. All this is at once desirable, but there is a problem—it is the self.

Jesus Christ loves; He is good and complete. God desires that those He has called be conformed to the likeness of His Son. He has predestined it to be so. People are self-reliant; they want to live their own lives according to their own way. The natural man, the strength of nature, is strong—to give up the self-life is most difficult.

God is the God of Abraham and Isaac but also the God of Jacob. Jacob knew the always present and comforting Holy Spirit whose training and discipline are the means of annihilation and transfiguration. God's ways are perfect. Know God as Jacob knew Him…

GOD

4

Know the God of Jacob

"And we, who with unveiled faces all reflect the Lord's glory, are being transformed into his likeness with ever increasing glory, which comes from the Lord, who is the Spirit."

2 Corinthians 3:18

Crucified with Christ, a person has been released from the bondage of sin. Born of God, one has new life in Christ. The indwelling Christ answers all that is needed for life and godliness. Why are there Christians who are defeated, ineffective, and unproductive? Why are there children born of God who bear very little resemblance to their Father or to Christ the Son? It is because of the natural man. Jacob's life points to the Holy Spirit and His work of transforming the natural man into the likeness of Christ.

God saw all He had created and declared it good. Man, fearfully and wonderfully made, is blessed with brainpower, physical strength, creative genius, and gifted with abilities. A person can set goals and succeed. People build bridges, erect skyscrapers, invade space, and can be seen and heard round the world and beyond. They accomplish great things and create beauty. History and the present are testimony to man's ingenuity and his outstanding achievements.

Endowed with all these attributes and powers, what is the problem with the natural man? He is of the earth. He has Adam's propensity to live independent of God. Self-reliant and able, a person trusts in his own strengths and is reluctant to rely on God, but the natural man cannot attain God's high standard of holiness and purity. Left to his own devises, he makes a mess of himself and his world.

The natural man is often proud, arrogant, and boastful. Human nature tends to be selfish, and self is often rude, offensive, and unkind. Man, by his very nature, does not want to deny himself or die daily, but there is no other way for the life of Christ to be revealed in him. "For we who are alive are always being given over to death for Jesus' sake, so that his life may be revealed in our mortal body" (1 Corinthians 4:11). The discipline of the Holy Spirit forges a thoroughfare through the hard soil of natural man so that the life of Christ within has a way out.

God's purpose is three-fold: to teach believers to rely on God as their strength, to rely on Christ as their life, and to transform the natural man to the likeness of Christ. Creation is not equal. Some are born with few talents and abilities while others are gifted. Most have average intelligence while others are brilliant. Families and places of birth are widely diverse. Poverty, ill health, or faulty parenting may deprive some of self-confidence. The privileged may be dauntless and self-assured. There is disparity, but God's three-fold purpose remains the same for all who are called by His name.

Jacob was born with a great ability and determination to achieve and excel. Some speak disparagingly of him because of his cunning, but like the rest of humanity, he was fallible and faulty. Who can know his errors? Jacob's life is an account of the Holy Spirit's work in his life to achieve God's three-fold purpose.

Jacob's Troubles

Jacob's trouble began in the womb. He struggled with Esau to be born first, but was born last holding onto Esau's heel. For this, they named him Jacob—one who supplants. Young Jacob knew about God's promise to Abraham and the heritage that had passed to Isaac. With all his heart, he wanted to be next in line, but Esau had the birthright. Jacob, who loved being at home, had prepared some wonderfully fragrant stew. Esau, an outdoorsman, came in from hunting faint and famished, and said, "Give me some of that stew." Jacob, seeing his advantage, answered, "First, sell me your birthright." Esau sold his birthright.

Years later Isaac called Esau to give him the blessing of the first-born, but Jacob, by cunning and deception, convinced his nearly blind father that he was Esau and received the blessing. For a single meal, Esau sold his inheritance rights as the elder son. When he wanted to receive the blessing, he was passed over. Visibly shaken, Isaac asked, "Why have you deceived me?" Isaac had not been allowed to bless the one God had rejected. By cunning, Jacob obtained the birthright and the blessing, but what he got for his scheming was an angry brother who threatened to kill him, and now Jacob has to leave. No longer are the tents of his wealthy father home. Here he has lived in security and plenty, the favored son of a doting mother. Jacob, it seems, desired the birthright and the blessing, but God Himself was not sought. The discipline of the Holy Spirit has begun.

Rebekah, Jacob's mother, advised Jacob to go to Haran and stay with her brother until Esau's anger waned. Isaac counseled him to choose a wife from relatives who lived there. Jacob left home on foot with only his staff. He traveled all day. Nighttime darkness fell over the land—and over Jacob's spirit. He is tired, weary, discouraged, and homeless. Here now, God's purpose is not on hold. Jacob is exactly where God wants him.

In Genesis 28:12-15, Jacob lay down using a stone for a pillow and slept. Dreaming, he saw a ladder extending from earth to heaven with angels ascending and descending. Above it stood the Lord who said, "I am the Lord, the God of your father Abraham and the God of Isaac. I will give you and your descendants the land on which you are lying. Your descendants will be like the dust of the earth, and you will spread out to the west and to the east, to the north and to the south. All peoples on earth will be blessed through you and your offspring. I am with you and will watch over you wherever you go, and I will bring you back to this land. I will not leave you until I have done what I have promised you." Wow!

Jacob wakens and realizes "the Lord is in this place." He is afraid and thinks, "This is the house of God, the gate of heaven, an awesome place" (Genesis 28:17). Early the next morning Jacob took the stone he had used for a pillow and set it up as a pillar. He poured oil on it and called the place Bethel. Listen to what he says: "If God will be with me and will watch over me on this journey I am taking and will give me food to eat and clothes to wear so that I may return safely to my father's house, then the Lord will be my God and this stone that I have set up as a pillar will be God's house, and of all that you give me I will give you a tenth" (Genesis 28:21-22). How human; God has given him glorious, unconditional promises, and Jacob is concerned with food and raiment. How like Jacob to want to bargain—if God will, then I will. Nonetheless, Jacob has had an encounter with God. The immanent Holy Spirit will be with him, will watch over him, and will not leave him.

God's plan for a people of His own through whose seed the world would be blest began with Abraham. The purpose of Jacob's life is to further this plan. This is most serious because Jacob cannot do God's business by his own powers. Many of his problems came from trying to fulfill the purpose of God by his own ingenuity. God has a purpose for every life, but to succeed according to God's measure, one must rely on Him. If, like Jacob, a person depends on himself and his natural abilities to accomplish God's purpose, the Holy Spirit will begin to weaken a person's confidence in that which he depends on rather than God. One may continually find himself in uncomfortable situations and adverse circumstances, which the Holy Spirit will use to lessen his independence and show him his need to rely on God. Such is the discipline of the Holy Spirit.

Jacob's lonely journey ends when he arrives in Haran. His uncle Laban meets him and welcomes him into his home. After about a month of hospitality, Laban, who could bargain and scheme as shrewdly as Jacob, decided theirs should be a business relationship. Jacob must work. Laban asked, "What shall I pay you?" Laban has two daughters, Leah and Rachel. Jacob is in love with Rachel and said, "I will work for you seven years for Rachel" (Genesis 29:18).

Seven years pass and Jacob asks for Rachel. After a great feast and celebration, Jacob retired to his tent and did not know until the next morning that Laban had sent Leah to him instead of Rachel. This was a devastating shock and memory stirred when Jacob asked, "What have you done to me, why have you deceived me?" Laban answered, "It is not the custom to give a younger daughter in marriage before the older one. If you will finish the bridal week with Leah, you can also have Rachel, but you have to work another seven years to pay for her" (Genesis 29:26-27).

Jacob's troubles continue—there is jealousy between the sisters over child bearing and because Rachel is the one loved. Leah bore Jacob four sons. Rachel, not bearing children, gave Jacob her maidservant Bilhah to have children for her. Bilhah bore two sons. When Leah stopped having children, she gave her maidservant Zilpah to Jacob and Zilpah had two sons. Leah had two more sons and a daughter. Rachel finally conceived and gave birth to a son she named Joseph.

Fourteen years have passed and Jacob now has eleven sons and one daughter. After Joseph is born, Jacob's heart turns toward home, so he said to Laban, "Give me my wives and my children for whom I have worked, and I will be on my way." Laban urged him to stay saying, "The Lord has blessed me while you are with me." Jacob replied, "The Lord has blessed you, but when may I do something for my own household?" They bargained, and Jacob said, "I will continue tending your flocks, but all the streaked, speckled, and spotted goats and dark lambs will be mine." Jacob had had a dream indicating that God would increase these animals. Jacob, true to form, went to a lot of trouble peeling branches and placing them in strategic places, trusting in his own cleverness to help God fulfill His promise. God did increase Jacob's flocks. Modern experiments have found Jacob's method to be ineffective. He also contrived, by husbandry, to manipulate the breeding so the weak animals would go to Laban.

Homeward Bound

Jacob worked for Laban six more years and prospered exceedingly. Laban's attitude changed toward him. God spoke, telling Jacob to go back to the land of his birth. Fearing Laban would strip him of his family and belongings, he fled surreptitiously. With his family on camels and driving his livestock ahead of him along with all the goods he had accumulated, Jacob left Haran.

Laban, feeling cheated, called his relatives together and pursued him with evil intent. He caught up with him in Gilead where Jacob had set up camp. God had warned Laban in a dream not to say anything good or bad to Jacob, nevertheless, Laban railed at Jacob, "Why did you deceive me and leave secretly? You have been foolish. I can harm you. Leah and Rachel are mine, the grandchildren are mine, the flocks are mine, all you have is mine." Jacob reminded him, "I have been with you twenty years now. Your sheep have not miscarried nor have I eaten rams from your flocks. I did not bring you animals torn by wild beasts; I bore the loss myself. And you demanded payment from me for whatever was stolen by day or night. I worked for you fourteen years for your two daughters and six years for your flocks, and you changed my wages ten times. If the God of my father had not been with me, you surely would have sent me away empty-handed. But God has seen my hardship and the toil of my hands, and last night he rebuked you." Jacob sacrificed to the Lord and prepared a meal for all. Laban and Jacob made a pact that neither would harm the other, and Laban returned home.

Jacob, continuing on his journey, was met by angels—this was the camp of God, and he did not need to be afraid. He called the place Mahanaim, which means two companies. Jacob sent messengers to his brother Esau to say, "Jacob, your servant, is coming home and hopes to find favor in his master's sight."

The messengers returned saying, "Esau is coming to meet you with four hundred men." In fear and distress, Jacob divided his people and animals into two groups. If Esau attacked one group, the other might escape. Jacob, reminding God of His promises, prayed, "I am unworthy of all the kindness and faithfulness you have shown your servant. I had only my staff when I crossed this Jordan, but now I have become two groups. Save me, I pray, from the hand of my brother Esau."

Jacob prayed this desperate, meaningful, humble prayer, but like many who pray but have little faith in God or His promises, he put forth his own elaborate and expensive plan. Jacob selected huge numbers of male and female goats, rams and ewes, camels with their young, cows and bulls, and male and female donkeys. He put them in the care of his servants, each herd by itself. The servants were sent ahead and told to keep some distance between the herds. As each one met Esau and was asked, "to whom do you belong?" he was to say, "to your servant Jacob. These are a gift sent to my lord Esau, and he is coming behind us." Maybe these gifts would pacify his brother and he would not harm him.

Eventide, Jacob sent his family and possessions across the ford of the river Jabbok, and he was alone. His troubles had begun when he found himself a poor, lonely vagabond. They continued at the hands of his uncle Laban who deceived him regarding Rachel and who was a hard taskmaster. For twenty years, Jacob tended Laban's sheep. Heat consumed him by day and cold by night so that sleep fled from his eyes, and Laban changed his wages at will. One may think all this hardship had little effect on Jacob for he was still a schemer, but God had begun a good work in him. That night a man wrestled with him until daybreak. When He could not overpower Jacob, He touched the socket of his hip so it was wrenched out of place. The thigh adverts to strength. This crippling touch of love was couched in penetrating reality—God is his strength. Know the God of Abraham.

The divine wrestler could have easily overcome Jacob, but the truth here is spiritual. He could not overpower him because Jacob would not surrender. Man has been given free will, and Jacob would not give up his right to himself, his self-reliance, his self-life. Man's natural strengths are not at issue, but rather a person's dependence on them instead of God. God is the source of strength; rely on Him and life's purpose is realized.

God's touch awakens a person to what he is. When asked his name, he confessed he was Jacob, a deceiver. Jacob could no longer wrestle, but he could cling and say, "I will not let you go unless you bless me." The wrestler would not give His name, but He gave Jacob a new name, "Your name will no longer be Jacob but Israel, because you have struggled with God and with men and have overcome" (Genesis 32:28).

Jacob had surrendered. The touch that taught him his strength is in God and not in himself made him an overcomer. The limp, the divine wound, is his testimony. Jacob became aware of three things: he had seen God face to face, he limped, and he had a new name. This is new life, life to live by. Know the God of Isaac.

Jacob, shaken and weak from a night of wrestling, limping and confused, is still afraid. Jacob is changed, but Esau is coming with four hundred men. In fear, he divides his family putting the most favored in the rear. He went on ahead and bowed seven times toward his brother, but Esau ran and embraced him, threw his arms around him and kissed him, and they wept. God is faithful. Jacob and his family are safe.

Jacob's Sorrows

Canaan, Jacob's homeland, is finally set upon. He bought a plot of ground in sight of Shechem where he built an altar. Jacob is beset by many sorrows. Dinah, his only daughter, is defiled. To avenge the wrong done to their sister, Jacob's sons slaughter the Shechemites. In grave danger from the surrounding peoples, the threat of annihilation is real. With no schemes of his own, Jacob and his family set out from there, and the terror of God fell upon all the towns around them so no one pursued them.

They traveled to Luz. Here Jacob built an altar to worship the Lord, for it was here that God had first revealed Himself to him. God appeared to him again and blessed him, reminding him that he is no longer Jacob, but is now Israel. The land promised to Abraham and Isaac would be his and his descendants. Jacob set up a stone pillar at the place where God had talked to him and poured a drink offering and oil on it. Jacob called the place Bethel.

Moving on toward Ephrath, later called Bethlehem, Jacob's beloved Rachel died giving birth to her second son, Benjamin. More sorrow came to him as he moved on. Reuben, his first-born, wronged him by sleeping with Bilhah, his concubine. Jacob came home to Hebron. Rebekah, his mother, was already dead. Sometime later his father, Isaac, died. Hebron is where Abraham and Isaac had sojourned and the place Jacob called home. It is here that Joseph, his best-loved son, is taken from him by the treachery and deceit of his other sons. Believing Joseph to be dead, Jacob grieves and cannot be comforted.

Years later, a severe famine ravishes the land. Jacob's wealth is threatened because his wealth is in livestock, now at risk for lack of food.

After hearing there is a plenteous supply in Egypt, all Jacob's sons, except Benjamin, go there to buy grain. Joseph, now governor of Egypt, recognizes his brothers, but wanting to know their hearts, speaks harshly, questions them about family, and treats them as spies. To prove their sincerity, Joseph holds Simeon as a prisoner until they return with Benjamin, their other brother. Time passes and they are again out of grain. Those Jacob loved most are gone, all who are left and all he has worked for are in impending peril. Now Benjamin, his heart, his last link with Rachel, must also be given up. With much trepidation and sorrow, Jacob let Benjamin go.

Mature and Complete

God touched Jacob at Peniel and changed his name to Israel. He came to Succoth in Canaan—a time of weakness, uncertainty, and confusion as he learned to walk, no longer in the strength of his own nature, but with a limp and in total reliance on God.

Jacob came to Shechem, the place of learning. He traveled on to Bethel where God had first appeared to him. God spoke to him again and there he built an altar and worshiped. Leaving Bethel, he came home to his father in Hebron, the place of fellowship. These places identify Canaan. At Shechem, one learns that in God only are righteousness and strength. Come to Bethel, it is by worshiping one learns that God is his life. Experience Hebron. It is by fellowship and beholding that one reflects the Lord's glory and that transformation into His likeness becomes a reality. This is the road Abram traveled to become Abraham, the road Jacob traveled to become Israel.

In his later years, Jacob is a gentle, winsome, and loving man. The Holy Spirit has done His work. Jacob at one time had put the least favored in the forefront of danger. Now, though Simeon and Levi had put them all at risk and knowing Reuben had wronged him, he is nevertheless concerned about the safety and well-being of the sons shepherding the flocks. He sent Joseph to see about them. When Joseph came to them, out of hatred and jealousy, they sell him to the Midianites and bring home an evil report about his death. Jacob's reaction is one of total brokenness. Years later, when faced with having to let Benjamin go, he said, "If it must be, take him with you…And may God Almighty grant you mercy before the man so that he will let your other brother and Benjamin come back with you. As for me, if I am bereaved, I am bereaved" (Genesis 43:14). Nothing is his, his confidence is in God and his transactions are with Him.

Assured that Joseph is alive and a man of great power in Egypt, Jacob, in joy and deep longing, said, "I will go and see him before I die." All the family with all their possessions set out for Egypt. They came to Beersheba, Canaan's southern border where Jacob stopped to sacrifice and inquire of the Lord. Could he go to Egypt even to see his most beloved son and ease his broken heart?

Canaan is the land promised to his descendants. Abraham had been called to this land and each time he left it, he found himself in trouble. Isaac had started to Egypt, and the Lord had stopped him. God appeared to Jacob in a vision and said, "Do not be afraid to go down to Egypt for I will make you into a great nation there. I will go down to Egypt with you and I will surely bring you back again. And Joseph's own hand will close your eyes" (Genesis 46:3-4).

Joseph's story begins and Jacob retires into the background. Jacob is now seldom seen, but Joseph, a type of Christ (seen suffering and then reigning in power and glory) is in the forefront. In life, may self be seldom seen that the life of Jesus may be revealed.

See Israel in the court of Pharaoh. The Jacob of old, scheming and conniving, could have found many ways to take advantage of Joseph's high position, or he might have been servile as he was with Esau, but not Israel. Israel came before Pharaoh with no pretense. He was a pilgrim. And Jacob said to Pharaoh, "My years have been few and difficult and they do not equal the years of the pilgrimage of my fathers" (Genesis 47:9). Yet he blessed Pharaoh. "And without doubt the lesser person is blessed by the greater" (Hebrews 7:7). Israel, in humility and dignity, blessed Pharaoh.

Israel is dying. The important things he recalls to Joseph are that God had appeared to him at Bethel with wonderful promises and that Rachel, to his sorrow, died while they were still on the way to Hebron. Joseph brings his two sons to him and Jacob blesses them. Isaac, in his old age, was about to bless the wrong son, but Israel, though almost blind as Isaac had been, is very much aware that his blessing is according to the will of God. In godly wisdom and insight, he prophesies over each of his own sons. Israel mature and complete dies blessing others and worshipping God

The Holy Spirit

After many hardships and losses, the Holy Spirit has taught Jacob that God is his strength and his life, but scripture reveals more of Jacob. His life is about transformation. The work of the Holy Spirit is represented by precious stones. Precious stones, developed by heat and pressure, dug and hacked out of hard earth, are cut and polished to make them things of beauty. Such was the life of Jacob. This independent and conniving natural man, after being wrought upon by the Holy Spirit, has become transparent, gentle, and gracious. He who began a good work in Jacob has carried it on to completion. Jacob, one who supplants, has become Israel, one who prevails—a prince.

A woman may die in childbirth. Loved ones pass on, children may be taken away, some disappoint. Economies face downturns and nature can be destructive; security is threatened. At times life is at risk. It is not what happens but how one deals with what happens that identify a person. God uses the circumstances of life to fashion a vessel of honor.

If storm tossed, trust the Lord. "I will build you with stones of turquoise, your foundations with sapphires. I will make your battlements of rubies, your gates of sparkling jewels, and all your walls of precious stones" (Isaiah 54:12). Like Jacob, those trained by the Holy Spirit may have known hardship and suffering, but they have become strong in the Lord and bear a conspicuous resemblance to Christ. "And we, who with unveiled faces all reflect the Lord's glory, are being transformed into his likeness with ever increasing glory, which comes from the Lord who is the Spirit" (2 Corinthians 3:18).

Jacob knew God as the immanent Holy Spirit, the One who leads and guides, the Paraclete who said, "I will not leave you until I have done what I have promised you" (Genesis 28:15). God watched over him at Gilead. The angels of God met him at Mahanaim. At a lonely spot in Peniel, God wrestled with him and changed his name to Israel. God protected him from disaster at Shechem. He traveled on to Bethel and God spoke to him there. Then he came to Hebron, his name had been changed to Israel, but it was here that he became Israel. The Spirit led Jacob and protected him on this long journey from Haran to Hebron. God made Himself known all along the way. Later, the Holy Spirit directed him to Egypt and confided His plan to him.

Look ahead to the wilderness tabernacle. The High Priest wore a breastpiece with the brilliance of the Urim, meaning light, and the perfection of the Thummin, having to do with truth. Worn over his heart, the breastpiece "will always be the means of making decisions for the Israelites…before the Lord" (Exodus 28:30). "Send forth your light and your truth, let them guide me" (Psalm 43:3a). Those led by the Spirit are the children of God; they walk in light and truth.

God calls Himself the God of Abraham, the God of Isaac, and the God of Jacob. If Abraham, in some limited way, is a type of God and Isaac a type of Christ, then it follows that Jacob is a type of the Holy Spirit. God appeared to Jacob at Bethel and Jacob set up a rock as a memorial and poured oil on it. This is most profound. No one else in scripture poured oil on a rock. In this, Jacob is a type of the Holy Spirit who anointed Christ. Christ, meaning the anointed one, is spoken of as the "Rock." As Jacob came into Bethel the second time, God appeared to him, and Jacob set up another memorial rock. This time he poured a drink offering and oil on it. This typifies the Holy Spirit and the unspeakable joy on the day of Pentecost when God poured out His Spirit.

Soon after this event in Bethel, Benjamin is born and now with twelve sons, the nation of Israel comes into view. Here again, Jacob typifies the Holy Spirit. With the outpouring of the Holy Spirit, the Church of Jesus Christ is born, and the reign of grace begins. It is interesting to note that Jacob's first ten sons represent the Jewish nation and the administration of Law. Then Joseph is born, a type of Christ, and after him, Benjamin, representing grace and this age of grace in which we all live because of Christ the sacrifice.

GOD

5

Christ the Sacrifice

"God himself will provide the lamb
for the burnt offering..."

Genesis 22:8

"John saw Jesus...and said,
Look, the Lamb of God,
who takes away the sin of the world."

John 1:29

Christ is the atoning sacrifice for the sins of mankind; this is blessed assurance for the Christian. Consider now the sacrifice of Christ in its fullness. The Levitical sacrifices foreshow what was accomplished at Calvary and its all-encompassing sufficiency. Leviticus is often thought to be a record of antiquated Jewish customs having no message for today, but the completeness and efficacy of Christ as the perfect sacrifice of God is vividly portrayed in these five Jewish offerings.

Reflect on Jesus Christ as the antitype and one looks with wonder and awe at the accuracy, precision, and detail of the prototype. Viewed against the backdrop of the New Testament and the life and crucifixion of Christ, it is clear that no one ritualistic sacrifice could convey Calvary in its fullness and preponderance of meaning. Animals without blemish, the sacrifices of the Old Testament, foreshadowed the life and death of Christ. If Christ is not discerned in the Old Testament with its varied and many types and shadows, much of the truth and richness of scripture is not understood.

The Burnt Offering

A burnt offering was sacrifice of the highest order because it foreshadowed Christ, without spot or defect, offering Himself to God. Christ in the burnt offering was exclusively for the eyes and heart of God. Only God could fully appreciate the cross as an expression of perfect love and devotion. If man had not sinned, there would be no need for sacrifice, but the burnt offering does not foresee Christ on the cross as sin-bearer. It reveals Christ accomplishing the will of God for the glory of God. Calvary gives voice to Christ's love for the Father in a language that only the Father could hear and understand.

Burnt offerings were voluntary. A male without defect from the herd or flock was sacrificed. Christ, who fulfilled the type, said, "The reason the Father loves me is that I lay down my life—no one takes it from me, but I lay it down of my own accord" (John 10:17). The person bringing the offering was imperfect, but placing his hand on the unblemished animal deemed him as perfect as the sacrifice. Those who receive Christ as their Savior are accepted by God, blameless and beyond reproach.

The sacrifice was cut in pieces and the legs and inner parts washed to show their perfection. Outwardly and inwardly, the animal was without defect. Jesus Christ, in whom there is no sin, committed no sin. He was incorruptible and true, immaculate and pure.

Aaron's sons, clothed in selected garments and performing their duties at the altar, are there to behold the flame of a perfect sacrifice rise to God as a sweet savor. Aaron's sons represent all who, clothed in robes of righteousness, worship the God of heaven for the sacrifice of His Son.

Accepted because of its perfection and cleanness, the burnt offering was totally consumed on the altar. It ascended as perfume of rare and sacred vintage to God the Father. Burnt offerings foreshadowed Christ offering Himself to God. Here was no sin-bearing and no wrath. All who have known that Christ died for sinners are silenced by the ineffable and pure love of the Son for the Father as revealed in the burnt offering—the Son who came to do the will of His Father and became obedient unto death, even death on a cross.

The Grain Offering

Christ and the perfection of His life are presented in a very clear manner in the grain offerings. These were sweet-savor offerings, and there was no bloodshed but rather a picture of the unsullied manhood of Jesus as He lived, served, and walked on earth. Elements used in the grain offering, and how they were presented, give understanding to the significance of the type. Grain ground fine was the basis; there must be no coarseness or unevenness in the flour—the shadow of the faultless Son of God passes before one in the meaning of the fine flour. Christ Jesus, who was righteous in all His ways, could say, "Come unto me all you who labor and are heavy laden" (Matthew 11:28) and in the same evenness of spirit, rebuke the self-righteous. He could, without meanness of spirit, say to Peter, "Get behind me, Satan, you are a stumbling block to me" (Matthew 16:23) then, with the same high order of merit, wash Peter's feet. Christ, the only perfect man who ever lived, neither sinned nor made mistakes. He never had to recall a word, retract a statement, or retrace a step.

Oil, representing the Holy Spirit, was mingled with the fine flour and spread or poured on baked or grilled cakes. Jesus, the antitype, was filled with the Spirit and anointed by the Spirit. Oil speaks of the power of His ministry. God the Son—being made in human likeness—did His teaching, preaching, and miracles by the power of the Holy Spirit.

Frankincense, always brought with a grain offering, denoted the object of Christ's ministry; He did everything to the glory of God. The priest took a handful of the offering and all the frankincense to burn a memorial portion to God, a pleasing aroma. Jesus was a guiltless, self-emptied, obedient man doing the will of God for the glory of God. His unsullied excellence came before the throne of Heaven as incense.

Salt was required in the grain offerings. "Season all your grain offerings with salt. Do not leave the salt of the covenant of your God out of your grain offerings; add salt to all your offerings" (Leviticus 2:13). In this ancient eastern culture, sharing salt with another was emblematic of fidelity and friendship. God made a covenant with Israel; He would be their God and they must worship Him only. They would be His people and if true to Him, Israel would be His treasured possession. Salt has purifying and preserving qualities. A new covenant, "I will put my law in their minds and write it on their hearts. I will be their God and they will be my people" (Jeremiah 31:33b) is penned with the blood of Christ to make His people pure and preserved unto life eternal.

Honey and leaven were forbidden in grain offerings. Honey denotes worldly pleasures and things or persons loved more than God. Leaven refers to sin. Christ is clearly portrayed; His love for God was the dynamic of His sinless life.

Inordinate affections and sin supplant peace of mind and enjoyment of God. It is unholy for a Christian to be tainted by the honey and leaven of this world while lacking the frankincense of worship and the salt of fidelity.

All grain offerings were prepared according to specified ways and baked in an oven or on a griddle. If just plain grain was brought, crushed heads of new grain roasted in the fire were offered. Crushing, heat, and fire suggest suffering. Christ was a man of sorrows and acquainted with grief. He suffered in His righteous soul because of the hypocrisy, wickedness, cruelty, and hatred He encountered. A corrupt cursed world is replete with sickness, pain, sorrow, and death—Jesus wept. Anticipating the cup He was to drink, becoming sin, and taking upon Himself the sins of the whole world, His suffering was so intense His sweat was like drops of blood.

After the memorial portion and the frankincense were burned as an offering to God, the rest was given to the priest and his sons. It was eaten in a holy place because it was most holy. The memorial portion and the priests' share were of the same offering. It satisfied God, and it satisfied His servants. The priest and his sons indicate spiritual strength and energy. They typify the worshipping church feeding upon the perfections of Christ Jesus with whom God is well pleased. Christ is clearly pictured in the grain offering.

The Fellowship Offering

Fellowship was the purpose of creation! God came to the garden paradise in the cool of the day and called, "Where are you?" Adam and Eve had sinned and in great fear hid among the trees. God, who knows everything, had not come in anger. The curse was the unavoidable consequence of their sin, but love brought Him to the garden. He had come for fellowship, but now those He loved were lost, undone, ruined, and separated from Him. God wanted them.

Sin made Adam and Eve aware of their nakedness and need to be clothed. The fig leaf coverings they had made represented self-righteousness and were not acceptable. God saw their need and made coverings for them from animal skins. Blood was shed, foretelling Calvary, and again there could be communion. It's about fellowship.

Fellowship offerings were sweet-savor offerings. Here again is no sin bearing. An unblemished animal from the herd or the flock, male or female, could be brought. Here, male or female does not refer to gender, but to strength and the broad scope of those who may fellowship. A Christian, whether spiritually strong or weak, has access to God because of Christ the sacrifice.

The dominate thought of the fellowship offering is communion. Its significance is forced upon the mind and heart when at Christ's death the curtain separating the presence of God from His people was torn asunder from top to bottom.

All the burnt offering was consumed in the fire, but in the fellowship offering, only a memorial portion was burned. The inner fat, the kidneys, and the covering of the liver, the richest parts were offered to

God, a sweet-savor offering. Signifying love and strength, the breast and a thigh, the parts that best suit man, were given to the priest and his family who were ritually clean. The priests worshipped as spectators at the burnt offerings, but as participators at the fellowship offerings. They shared in the sacrifice offered to God. Worshippers in fellowship with each other, enjoying Christ, and partaking of His love and strength, are clearly pictured in the fellowship offering. Christ, loved by the Father, is loved and worshipped by His people.

After the memorial portion and the priests' share were offered, the worshipper had the rest of the sacrifice to eat in celebration with family and friends who were ceremonially clean. Remember the prodigal son who returned home a poor tatterdemalion. He was not left in his ragged, filthy garment, nor was it washed and repaired. His father provided a new robe. Ponder the sinner. He is corrupt, unclean, and beyond repair. He is dead. God has provided new life.

This is a celebration. They killed the fatted calf. The father brought the prodigal adorned in the best robe, a ring on his finger, and sandals on his feet to his own table to feed on the fattened calf in fellowship with him. He who was loved, lost, and yearned for is found. Hear the lyrics of the fellowship offering, "we had to celebrate and be glad" (Luke 15:32).

An angry, unforgiving, and jealous elder brother refused to celebrate. Sadly, he had never been stirred by his father's love and fellowship, "you are always with me," nor had he grasped the truth of "everything I have is yours."

Fellowship offerings were often brought as an expression of thanksgiving. Along with the fellowship offering, a grain offering of various unleavened cakes was required. An unclean person concerning any of the Lord's ordinances could not eat of the offering, reminding one that there can be no sin or impurity in the presence of God. Nevertheless, cakes made with leaven, signifying sin also had to be offered. Here again, the outstanding accuracy of the Holy Spirit concerning the type and its application is noteworthy. Sin in the flesh, the sin nature inherited from Adam, contaminates all flesh. No one is denied access to God because of this sin in the flesh. It has been atoned for by the sin offering ere one could bring a fellowship offering.

Is there any passion to know God, a yearning that speaks? "As the deer pants for streams of water, so my soul pants for you, O God. My soul thirsts for God, for the living God. When can I go and meet with God?" (Psalm 42:1-2). The fellowship offering answers this longing. All the claims of God are satisfied by Christ foreshadowed in the burnt offering and grain offering. Christ, the sin offering and guilt offering, meets all the needs of man. Christ, the sacrifice, has rent the curtain separating man from God. It's about fellowship.

The Sin Offering

Sin offerings were necessary "when anyone sins unintentionally and does what is forbidden in any of the Lord's commands…"(Leviticus 4:2). Man is a sinner by birth. He inherited this nature from Adam and sins because he is a sinner. Sin offerings atoned for this. In the Levitical economy, there were laws and many ordinances to be performed and commands to be obeyed. Persons living under the law could surely relate to the person portrayed in Romans 7 who, trying to please God according to the flesh said, "I have the desire to do what is good, but I cannot carry it out…When I want to do good, evil is right there with me" (Romans 7:19-21). Sin offerings had to be continually sacrificed because of this onslaught on the conscience.

Amazing grace! "…there is now no condemnation for those who are in Christ Jesus, because through Christ Jesus, what the law was powerless to do in that it was weakened by the flesh, God did by sending His own Son…to be a sin offering. And so he condemned sin in the flesh in order that the righteous requirements of the law might be fully met in us who do not live according to the flesh, but according to the Spirit" (Romans 8:1-4).

Sin offerings were determined by the reach of the offender's influence; therefore, a young bull was required for sin at the highest level. If a ruler sinned, a male goat was offered and a female goat or lamb if a member of the community sinned. The poor could bring doves or pigeons and the very poor could bring a handful of fine flour.

Animals brought for sin offerings must be without defect. Sin was being judged, but the sacrifice must be perfect for it represented Christ. A holy sacrifice, it was presented at the Tent of Meeting and slaughtered there. He who brought the offering laid his hands on its head to transfer his sin to the sacrifice. Although a sin offering, the sacrifice was highly esteemed for a memorial portion was burned on the brazen altar.

The priest and his sons were given the offerings whose blood had not been carried into the sanctuary. Only the males of the family shared in these offerings, again symbolizing strength. It took spiritual strength to partake of an offering that condemned the just and set the unjust free, that let the guilty live and killed the innocent—to understand that the punishment for sin is death. Reflect on the triumphant tragedy of the cross. The innocent was put to death that the sinner might live! Brood over the pain and infamy of Calvary and share in Christ's sufferings.

If an anointed priest sinned, bringing guilt on all the people or if the whole community sinned, this was most serious. Sin at this highest level required the sacrifice of a young unblemished bull. Three things were involved: God's dwelling place among them, worship, and the individual conscience; all depended on the blood. In the offering for this level of sin, some of the blood was taken into the Holy Place and sprinkled seven times in front of the curtain before the Lord. This secured Jehovah's relationship with His people and His dwelling in their midst. Some of the blood was put on the horns of the altar of fragrant incense, securing the worship of the assembly. The rest of the blood was poured out at the base of the altar of burnt offering, fully answering the claims of individual conscience. Efficacious and powerful, the blood of Jesus meets every demand.

After considering what was done with the blood and the memorial portion of the sacrifice for sin at the highest level, see now what was done with the animal. "But the hide of the bull and all its flesh, as well as the head and legs, the inner parts and offal—that is all the rest of the bull—he must take outside the camp…and burn it on a wood fire on the ash heap" (Leviticus 4:11-12). "The high priest carries the blood of animals into the Most Holy Place as a sin offering, but the bodies are burned outside the camp. And so Jesus also suffered outside the city gate to make the people holy through his own blood. Let us then go to him outside the camp, bearing the disgrace he bore. For here we do not have an enduring city, but we are looking for the city that is to come" (Hebrews 13:11-14). Christ's death procured a city on high for His people, but the place He died divests them of a city below. His suffering secured their entrance into heaven, but where He suffered alienates them from earth. How easy it is to fit into this world's scheme of things. Christ is despised and rejected. How can those called by His name belong to a rejected Christ and not be a rejected people? This is not the despair of defeat. It is the victory of discipleship.

On the Day of Atonement, a once-a-year event, a bull was sacrificed for a sin offering and a ram for a burnt offering. The high priest, bringing some of the bull's blood, was allowed to go behind the curtain into the Most Holy Place. Coming into this holiest of places, the high priest carried a golden censor of burning coals from the altar on which he burned two handfuls of fragrant incense. Smoke of the burning incense concealed the atonement cover, so he would not die. Blood from the sacrifice was sprinkled on the front of the atonement cover of the Ark of the Covenant and then in front of it. The Ark of the Covenant contained the Ten Commandments, a jar of manna, and Aaron's rod that budded. Here God appeared in a cloud and when He looked on the atonement cover, He saw the blood and not the people's rebellion against His law, His provision, and His authority.

In the burnt offering, the focus is on the perfection of the sacrifice. In the sin offering, the attention is on the hatefulness of sin. Eons past, before the earth was founded, in the divine councils of the eternal Trinity, the Son of God was crucified. He would be the necessary sacrifice; the bearer of this horrible thing called sin and would endure its appalling consequences. In the fullness of time, He became sin. He who knew no sin bore all the petty, sordid, and atrocious sins ever devised and committed by mankind. Jesus, the Son of God, was put to shame and humiliation, was falsely accused, mocked, and beaten. His appearance was disfigured beyond description, and His form marred beyond human likeness—then they crucified Him.

This wondrous God-man suffered physical wracking pain in His body, a heart broken and overladen with sorrow, and anguish in His righteous, incorruptible soul. His Father hid His face from Him. "I will forever lift my eyes to Calvary, to view the cross where Jesus died for me."[3]

The Guilt Offering

Man begins with God as a repentant sinner. His first encounter with holiness brings an awareness of the many sins he has committed. The guilt offering presaged Christ dying for the sins of mankind. Sins committed make one unclean. The blood of Christ, the guilt offering, has thoroughly cleansed the sinner of these sins.

There is a grave difference in sin in the flesh, the sin nature inherited from Adam, and sins of the flesh, sins one has committed. If, after salvation, a person sins and again has sin on his conscience, what happens? Sin cannot make its way into God's presence. It does not affect God's thoughts concerning His child nor does it hide Christ, the advocate, from His view. Conscience is a different matter, for a person may be troubled by guilt. Fellowship with God has been short-circuited, and there is no joy. What must one do? Confess. "If we confess our sins, he is faithful and just and will forgive us our sins" (1 John 1:9). O Joy!

People are prone to say, "I'm sorry" and beg God for forgiveness. Notably, this is a misunderstanding of scripture. Forgiveness can be asked for day after day and the conscience not be relieved; one need not ask God to be faithful and just. Confession and repentance is prescribed. "When I kept silent, my bones wasted away from my groaning all day long…Then I acknowledged my sin to you and did not cover up my iniquity. I said, I will confess my transgressions to the Lord—and you forgave the guilt of my sin" (Psalm 32:3-5). To confess is to acknowledge the wrong. Confession is good for the soul; therefore, confess your sins. Confess at the foot of the cross. The conscious is relieved, peace attained, and communion restored. It's about fellowship.

Lambs brought for guilt offerings had to be without blemish. These holy offerings were brought to the Tent of Meeting and slaughtered there. In the Levitical system, a guilt offering was required for actual

---
[3] Dottie Rambo, "He Looked Beyond My Faults And Saw My Need", song lyrics

wrongs committed against the holy things of God, or against another person. If a man had deranged his relationship with God, he must bring to the Lord—as a penalty—a ram without defect and of the proper value in silver. In this way, the priest made atonement for him.

Again, the precision of the Holy Spirit in recording the prototype is awe-inspiring. Silver speaks of redemption, and a penalty is unique to this sacrifice. There is a price to pay for sin; the penalty is death. "All have sinned and gone astray, each has turned to his own way, and the Lord has laid on Him the iniquity of all" (Isaiah 53:6). Christ died. It was the will of God the Father to cause Him to suffer and to make His life a guilt offering. The high and terrible cost of sin has been paid and with Him is full redemption.

God's holiness is offended in ways that finite man may not recognize or perceive. God's inflexible holiness cannot tolerate any sin. All sin, known or unknown, is punishable. Sin has been paid for according to God's standard of holiness; it has been judged and all the claims of God have been satisfied. Christ, by His life and death, has satisfied the demands of a Holy God and as sin bearer has met man's need of a redeemer.

If a man sinned and was unfaithful to the Lord by deceiving, defrauding, or stealing from his neighbor, he was guilty. God viewed sin against another person as sin against Himself. Full restitution had to be made by returning what had been stolen and adding a fifth of the value to it. Jesus said, "If you are offering your gift at the altar and there remember your brother has something against you, leave your gift there in front of the altar. First go and be reconciled to your brother, then come and offer your gift" (Matthew 3:23). Wrongs, for the sake of conscious and the rights of another, must be corrected. The claims of Christianity demand that conduct and righteousness concur. It is hypocrisy to profess salvation, to speak of sins forgiven, and not do right, to talk of love and be barren of its fruit.

It Is Finished

There is significance in the listing of the Levitical offerings. The fellowship offering is in the middle and is the focal point because the reason for the sacrifices was fellowship. From God's position, the sacrifice of His Son, as symbolized in the burnt offering and grain offering, met His demands. Yet there could be no fellowship. God is holy and a holy God is worshipped in a holy place; no sin or impurity finds its way into His presence. Man is sinful, undone, naked, unclean, and guilty. In Christ, God provided a guilt offering for man's sins and a sin offering for his condition. Clothed in the righteousness of Christ and accepted by God, the redeemed can behold in adoration the triumphant Christ.

When the law of the offerings was written, the fellowship offering was listed last for when it is finished, there is fellowship. Christ Jesus having offered Himself as the fulfillment of all the offerings cried out, "It is finished." Infinite in design and profound in type, the Levitical offerings reveal to a lost world God's pure love and the scope of His great salvation. God the Father, in incomprehensible love, gave His beloved and only Son. God the Son, manifesting the love of His Father, gave His life. It is finished!

Hear God's love refrain, "I have loved you with an everlasting love" (Jeremiah 31:3).

GOD

6

Divine Love

*"Many waters cannot quench love,
rivers cannot wash it away."*

Song of Songs 8:7

God is love. The divine nature those born of God have partaken of is love. "God has poured out his love into our hearts by the Holy Spirit, whom he has given us" (Romans 5:5). Infinite love, present in the heart, is known as Spirit. Deep calling to deep is the love of heaven calling to the Spirit of love shed abroad in the heart—if one is tuned in, he is privileged to hear. Listen to the heart. "By day the Lord directs his love, at night his song is with me" (Psalm 42:8a).

Love purifies the heart. Fidelity and love intermingle. Virtues abound when love is strong and vices abate. In full bloom, love strengthens character, enriches the soul, ennobles action, and radiates grace. Love is the old commandment, the new commandment, the great commandment, and the fulfillment of the law.

Love is paramount for love comes from God. When love prevails, it is the panacea for the ills of society. It is healing for torn hearts and shattered lives. Love bridges troubled, angry waters and overlooks wrongs. The power of divine love can transform the wretched into the beautiful and convert the wicked into the righteous.

Love for God

Love God. "Love the Lord your God with all your heart and with all your soul and with all your strength" (Deuteronomy 6:5). Humanly speaking, this is not possible. In the presence of infinite love—boundless, sacrificial, and dependable—to offer God one's faulty, finite love is inadequate and discomfiting. A person is enabled to love God with heart, soul, and strength by the power of the indwelling Holy Spirit.

This is a love affair. An all-consuming passion for God prevents the love of the world. The Spirit God caused to live within envies intensely for I belong to my lover and his desire is for me. I will sing of the one I love. His love is more pleasing than wine. His ointments are fragrant, and His words are sweet to my taste. Your love, O God, is better than life, draw me nearer, nearer to you...Love God by the power of the indwelling Spirit of love.

Love, called agape in the Greek of scripture, is not a feeling but an action. God's love is revealed by what He does. Human love is motivated by feelings, but agape, the Spirit of love indwelling, expresses itself by actions because that is its nature. Anything done as unto the Lord—a cup of cold water for the thirsty, bread for the hungry, a visit to the lonely—manifests a love for God. Love is something one does; it is a commitment, not a feeling. Evidence of loving God is to obey His word and do His will. "Whoever has my commands and obeys them, he is the one who loves me" (John 14:21). Love God by obeying His commands and doing the things that please Him.

The strength of commitment depends on a person's trust in God's love. "This is love: not that we loved God, but that he loved us" (1 John 4:10). At the last supper, Peter, feeling his love for Jesus with emotional fervor, declared that even if all others fell away, he never would. Yet, at the moment of crisis, he denied being His follower or even knowing Him. In contrast, John thought of himself as the disciple whom Jesus loved. At the crucifixion, he was at the foot of the cross receiving last-minute comfort.

God loves His children; He calls each one by name and watches over them. His ears are attentive to their cry for God has charged Himself with the desires and needs of those He has chosen. Each one's proper business is with himself—how he relates to and remains in God's boundless, dependable, forgiving love. Love God by abiding in His amazing love.

Love for Self

True self-love is not self-seeking, boastful, or prideful; this is self-aggrandizement. Self-love that is healthy, scriptural, and necessary has to do with self-value. Every person is a soul of great worth. Sin's curse has brought about sickness and disease, the malformation of soul and body, distorted concepts and reprobate thinking. Evil desires place no value on life, but nothing devalues the soul. The soul is the person—the mind, the emotions, and the will. Its value is intrinsic, present from birth.

What price does one put on his soul? If the whole world with all its wealth, its apparent and hidden treasures, could be wrapped in purest gold and tied with ribbons of finest silver, it would not be enough to purchase one person. The price God put on each one was the life of His Son.

Coming from a minister's family, the value of a soul was often referred to. "Preach the word lest souls be lost." As a young person, I often thought of souls as lost. Years later, in a letter about the value of a soul, I referred to someone as an exquisite, priceless treasure. Something hit my heart with a force I felt—I was one of these exquisite, priceless treasures. Having had long-standing feelings of inferiority, this was a shock. Reflecting on this, I became afraid. Was I responsible for something priceless? Self-love is based on valuing one's priceless soul. Whatever the cost, do not lose it. Give it to Jesus.

An erroneous concept of life and its purpose is problematic and injurious. Instead of embracing one's self with love, a person might condemn and reject the self. Aware of one's imperfections, his many mistakes and failures, how does a person love himself? Loving one's self has nothing to do with appearance, talent, personality, accomplishments, or the lack thereof. Genetics and nature determine the physical and inherited traits, but the inmost being is God created, God breathed. Self-love grasps the truth that man is God's creation and that the breath of God gives him life.

Moreover, everyone born is a word of God spoken with love and intent. Every life is a gift of God presented first to parents and then to others, giving life profound significance and purpose. Created life, man's inmost being, is an expression of God having infinite value. Love this self that is created with a spark of the divine, this self that is a word, a gift, and an expression of God. Such holy self-love is unrestrained. It is a healing balm for the wounds of life and the means to wholeness. These truths become real when one is born again.

Jesus Christ, the incarnate Son, is the Word of God and the Gift of God. Christ, the infinite Son, the radiance of God's glory, the exact representation of His being, is the expression of God. He came to earth from heaven, and His life of eternal value had depths of meaning and purpose. Man is finite and of the earth but the pattern is the same. Each one is a word of God spoken with meaning and is a gift of God given with purpose. Just as a painting is an expression of the artist and music an expression of the composer, God's creation of a person is an expression of Himself, giving life value. These indications are who a person is. Each one is a God-created life of great value having meaning and purpose. Love and value this priceless treasure.

Sin and evil have twisted, defaced, and so corrupted life that its value is often veiled. Earthiness, human nature, and wickedness have entombed much of life's beauty, its meaning, and purpose. Due to the bustling and rush of life, its pleasures and its many clamoring demands, life is often lived on the surface and in the market place. Sit alone. Sit in silence. Sit in darkness. Shut out the many disturbing and claiming thoughts. In total quietude and deep silence look within and meet one's self—a word of God, a gift of God, and an expression of God. Love God for the wonder of life. Love life for the wonder of God.

Love for Others

At times, in the circle of one's acquaintances and relations, there are people one does not like—irritating, offensive people. Believers are not required to like everybody, but they are commanded to love one another deeply from the heart. "Lord, I do not even like him, I don't like her either. I will do what love does, I will be kind, I will not be rude. If someone is in need, I will help but I cannot love him or her, or any of these senseless people, and really God—from the heart?" Oh! If a person gives all he possesses to the needy and even becomes a martyr—without love—nothing is gained.

Jesus, speaking of love, could say, "Be perfect, therefore, as your heavenly Father is perfect" (Matthew 5:48). He was not referring to finite love but to His perfect love poured into the human heart. Human love can never be faultless or reliable. God is love; rely on the source. Christ demonstrated love; rely on His life. The Spirit is the power of love; live by the Spirit. John was writing about love and loving others when he wrote, "in this world, we are like Him" (I John 4:17).

Isaiah records the Lord's meaning of a true fast, which is a clear picture of love in operation. Love does not put another in bondage. "…loose the chains of injustice and untie the cords of the yoke, to set the oppressed free and break every yoke" (Isaiah 58:6). Requirements and expectations forced on another by threatened loss of love and support create a chain of injustice and bondage. This method of control to satisfy personal desires and demands is often used in families, among friends and lovers, in the work place, and in politics. Love sets free. A yoke is a means of making another person do one's own bidding. Pure love is disinterested; it gives and does, but neither expects or demands something in return. Love does not maneuver to control another.

What is love? "Is it not to share your food with the hungry and to provide the poor wanderer with shelter—when you see the naked to clothe him…?" (Isaiah 58:10). Giving food, shelter, and clothing to those in need is an act of love. In the world at large, one might contribute to charities. In the sphere of one's own small world, there may be a friend, a church member, or a relative in need. "If anyone has material possessions and sees his brother in need but has no pity on him, how can the love of God be in him?" (1 John 3:17).

It is often within the family that love is most sorely tested and attitudes challenged. Love does "not turn away from your own flesh and blood" (Isaiah 58:7b). Is a family member in need of time and attention, of validation, a listening ear, and an understanding heart? Share the love! People at school and in the workplace are often unfair, unkind, and unfeeling. Coming home one should enter a place of sheltering warmth, of order and comfort, and find arms that hold. Provide the love! At times, a person may feel exposed and vulnerable; the love and support of family protects. Clothe with love!

Love will "…do away with the yoke of oppression…" (Isaiah 58:9b). Oppression is the injurious and abusive treatment of another by word or act. Let love prevail and there will be no pointing finger or malicious talk and never any violence. "A gentle answer turns away wrath, but a harsh word stirs up anger" (Proverbs 15:1). If family members spend themselves meeting the needs of each other, everyone's needs are met, and no one is oppressed.

Love is something one does. Words of love are substantiated by acts of love, and love for others is clearly expressed in parental love. Heartfelt, natural affection for their children gives parents some degree of understanding of God's love—His forgiveness, patience, bestowal, and training concerning His children. Writing to the Thessalonians, Paul speaks of a mother's love as being gentle, a love that is delighted to share herself, her time, and strength with her children. A father's love encourages, comforts, and urges his children to live lives worthy of the Lord. A godly father exhibits both strength and gentleness. "Nothing is so strong as gentleness. Nothing so gentle as real strength."[4]

God appointed the man to be the head of the family. This does not indicate he is smarter or more spiritual or that as a husband he

---

[4] Sir Francis DeSales

arbitrarily has his way. It requires him to lead in spiritual matters such as church attendance and family altar, to teach by word and example. God, speaking of Abraham, cited the role of the family head. "For I have chosen him, so that he will direct his children and his household to keep the way of the Lord by doing what is right and just" (Genesis 18:19). Many families have two working parents. Sometimes moms work and dads stay home. God's appointed roles have not changed. As spiritual leader, a man who loves God and family will build a spiritual ark of truth and righteousness to save his family.

Moral decay, lack of genuine commitments, and the breakdown of family values have given society an over-abundance of single parents. Foundations are being destroyed and children are at risk. Renewed hope and help come to those who remain faithful to God and true to His word. Godly love poured out will save the children. His love will sustain, give direction, and impart wisdom to the parent. God's love never fails.

Love forgives. "Bear with each other and forgive whatever grievances you may have against one another" (Colossians 3:13). It may be hard to forgive, especially if the offence was egregious. Rely on the source. An outstanding quality of divine love is its ability to forgive. An unforgiving spirit creates bondage. If one does not forgive a wrong, the pain of the injury is ever with him. The demand for retribution, the need for revenge, or harboring hatred consumes the life, robbing a person of peace, clarity of thought, and health. Cancel the debt and experience the resulting freedom of forgiving. To forgive is required, but there may be no ability or desire to relate or re-instate. Forgiveness has been accomplished when one can look into the heart and feel no lingering pain or anger.

Forgiving one's self is crucial. If a person does not forgive his own self, he may be bound by guilt, remorse, and self-hate. Why not let the same spirit of love and forgiveness be applied to one's self as to others? God forgives, and one is justified freely by His abundant provision of grace.

God's Love

Man is finite. How can he describe infinite love? The whole of scripture is a love story of God's love for humanity. "How priceless is your unfailing love! Both high and low among men find refuge in the shadow of your wings. They feast on the abundance of your house; you give them drink from your river of delights. For with you is the fountain of life; in your light we see light" (Psalm 36:7-8).

Calvary demonstrates God's love. For while all were yet sinners, Christ died for them. He bled and died in order to display, in view of a wondering world, God's unfathomable love. Divine love surpasses knowledge. Words fail…

> Could we with ink the ink the ocean fill
> And were the skies of parchment made.
> Were every stalk on earth a quill
> And every man a scribe by trade
> To write the love of God above would
> Drain the ocean dry.
> Nor could the scroll contain the whole
> Though stretched from sky to sky.
> O love of God how rich and pure,
> How measureless and strong.
> It shall forever more endure,
> The saints and angel's song. [5]

---

[5] Author unknown

GOD

7

It's About Fellowship

> "Here I am! I stand at the door and knock. If
> anyone hears my voice and opens the door,
> I will come in and eat with him, and he with me."
>
> Revelation 3:20

An amazing and awesome truth. God Almighty, the God of Glory, wants to fellowship with His people. For this reason, there is a no more pressing need than a right relationship with God. Sacrifice, offering, or service do not supersede or take the place of relationship. God's people, a worshipping people, fellowship with Him in assembly, in life, and in prayer.

Assembly Fellowship

Scenes of people gathering to worship Jehovah God are found throughout the Old Testament. Most of the New Testament was written to groups of people, a church established as a place of worship and fellowship. Freedom to assemble for worship is taken for granted in a free country. Christians are often hated and in some parts of the world are martyred. Because of this and the prevailing threat to freedom, it suddenly becomes a coveted and valued privilege. The Church of the living God proclaims His love and spreads the gospel of salvation though the times are perilous. The wicked freely strut about because what is vile is honored among men. Evil is considered good and good evil. The wicked shoot from the shadows at the upright in heart. What can the righteous do when the foundations are being destroyed? "Let us not give up meeting together, but let us encourage one another—and all the more as you see the day approaching" (Hebrews 10:25). Call upon Him while He is near. In good times and trying times, gather to worship. God inhabits the praises of His people. "Glorify the Lord with me, let us exalt his name together" (Psalm 34:3).

Praise and worship services of the present day often have loud music and constant movement—a grand celebration. As an octogenarian, I remember other worship services. Hands were raised in adoration and praise. Suddenly, there came a holy hush, then an ethereal, harmonious hum of worship rose heavenward in a diaphanous mist. Though only seven, the sense of "something other" and the wonder of the sound made a lasting impression. This happened on few and rare occasions. Another time of vivid recall happened when as a teenager I felt enshrouded by the mist and remember wishing the beauty of the sound would last forever. It was always so brief. "Ascribe to the Lord the glory due his name; worship him in the splendor of His holiness" (Psalm 29:2).

Fellowship in Life

Enoch walked with God. Brother Lawrence of the seventeenth century wrote of the practice of the presence of God. Jean Pierre de Caussade of the same era referred to walking with God as the sacrament of the present moment. God is present in the now. "He that dwelleth in the secret place of the most High shall abide under the shadow of the Almighty" (Psalm 91:1KJV). The secret place is not some mystical, cloistered place shut off from life. It is recognizing God in the dailiness and busyness of life. It is not concentrating on God instead of the job at hand; it is doing the job at hand as unto the Lord and relying on His help to do it right. "The Lord is with me, he is my helper" (Psalm 118:7).

There is an open line to heaven for conversation with God. This amazing privilege allows one to at once give thanks for blessings, for answered prayer, or to confess a sin or a wrong. One can proclaim, "O God, how good you are." He can pray for wisdom and help now or ask, "Where, O God, have I put what I cannot find." God may speak. Listen to the heart. The mind will rationalize and analyze, feelings are fleeting and undependable, and the will tends to lean toward the needs and wants of the flesh. Where did the voice come from? God speaks to the heart, to the innermost man. The mind understands, the emotions are stirred, and the will is prompted to obey.

God, who promised never to leave or forsake His own, is present in joy and sorrow, in suffering and in laughter. In every situation and circumstance He is "… the God who sees me" (Genesis 16:13).

> "God…is everywhere. Everything proclaims him to you; everything reveals him to you. He is by your side, over you, around you and in you. Here is his dwelling and yet you still seek him. Ah! You are searching for God, the idea of God in his essential being. You seek perfection and it lies in everything that happens to you—your suffering, your actions, your impulses are the mysteries under which God reveals himself to you. But he will never disclose himself in the shape of that exalted image to which you so vainly cling. … O, glorious celebration! Eternal bounty, God forever available, forever being received. Not in pomp or glory or radiance, but in infirmity, in foolishness, in nothingness. God chooses what human nature neglects, out of which he works his wonders and reveals himself to all souls who believe that is where they will find him."[6]

Fellowship in Prayer

How often is prayer reduced to "Dear God, thank you for everything, bless me and mine, do this and do that, thank you, Amen." Prayer, communion with God, is an exercise of the spirit. How often it

---

[6] Jean Pierre De Caussade: *The Sacrament of the Present Moment, pages 18 and 20*

becomes an outpouring of the flesh, the pleadings of a beggar beseeching an unwilling God to grant the things asked for. There is a tendency to begin prayer by bemoaning one's failures, inadequacies, and sins or to relieve stress with emotional harangue. If the need is desperate, a person might even shout at God, demanding an answer. God may hear and answer such prayers, but one has not communed with God. There has been no fellowship.

There is a most excellent way. Sins and the sinner have been dealt with at the cross. Prior to approaching God for fellowship, wrongdoing or defilement have been confessed. God is faithful and just to forgive, and one comes before Him in full assurance of sins forgiven and clothed in the righteousness of Christ.

Effective, fervent prayer is an activity of the spirit and necessitates self-forgetfulness. The mind may be troubled and the heart aching, a person may be in a panic and aware of the desperation of a situation. Concentrate on God—he is glorious and powerful, and all things are possible. Turn the eyes on self and there is imperfection and unworthiness, and doubts arise. Pray with the mind stayed on God and wonderful things happen to soul and body.

Scripture speaks of the Tabernacle, God's Dwelling, and the Sanctuary as places of fellowship. Worship in the Tabernacle. Commune in His dwelling—encompassed by the presence of the Holy Spirit, one is in God's dwelling. Celebrate God in His Sanctuary. Worship, commune, and celebrate—in any order, singly or intermingled, however the Spirit leads.

The protocol for worship is clearly demonstrated in the rituals performed by the priests of the wilderness tabernacle. Spoken of as the Tent of Meeting, the tabernacle was surrounded by a curtained outer court. Predominant in the outer court, standing in front of the tabernacle, was the brazen altar. Sacrifices were slain and blood was shed in the courtyard; burnt offerings and memorial portions were consumed by fire on the brazen altar. The mirrored laver containing the water of cleansing, signifying personal holiness, stood in front of the Tent of Meeting. If a priest of old entered the Holy Place having neglected his cleansing at the laver, he would die. Blood was shed and sins forgiven, but actions and choices are individual responsibilities. If the conscience is troubled because of personal wrongs, disobedience, or defilement, one cannot worship in spirit and in truth.

All that happened regarding the sacrifices, the brazen altar, and the mirrored laver assured the worshiper's safe passage into the tabernacle. The first room, the Holy Place, housed the table for the bread of the presence, the golden lampstand, and the golden altar of incense. Behind a curtain was the Holy of Holies where God appeared in a cloud. When Christ was crucified, the curtain separating the Holy Place from the Most Holy Place was supernaturally torn open from top to bottom. Walk up Calvary's mountain; see Christ crucified, linger, meditate, be astounded; "sometimes it causes me to tremble, tremble, tremble."[7]

Blood was shed and atonement made. The Holy Place! Behold the risen Christ! Jesus Christ is the atoning sacrifice; realize who He is and what He has done. In Him is life and His life gives light. His presence is the satisfying bread of heaven. Be enraptured with Him who is faithful and true, whose name is the Word of God, and on whose head are many crowns. "On His robe and on His thigh He has this name written KING OF KINGS AND LORD OF LORDS" (Revelation 19:6). Spontaneous praise erupts. The Holy of Holies! One falls speechless in the presence of infinite, infallible love! This is worship.

Exalt Christ in the Holy place. Self is set aside, forgotten; needs or wants are not mentioned. Do not speak of sin. Thinking of one's sins in this Holy Place is not humility but unbelief regarding the sacrifice. Do not let self intrude lest the glory fades and one falls short of the Holy of Holies, the habitation of God where all is love.

Cleansed from sin by the "blood of the Lamb," a person becomes a temple, a "tabernacle" of the Holy Spirit who lives in the inner man. This is a most holy place—crown Christ King and be overwhelmed by the pure love of God.

---

[7] Old spiritual, author unknown

Commune with God in His dwelling place. Encompassed by the Holy Spirit, one has come to God's palace—His dwelling. Enter His gates with thanksgiving. "This is the gate of the Lord through which the righteous may enter" (Psalm 118: 20). "I will enter and give thanks to the Lord" (Psalm 118: 9).

Come into His courts with praise. This is the garden of God, a joyous place. "My soul yearns, even faints for the courts of the Lord" (Psalm 84:2). Acknowledge the Spirit's nearness—this shadow of the Almighty. Thrilled by the presence of the Holy Spirit, one is captivated with Christ in the courts of the Lord. The heart sings Halleluiah! Hallelujah! Hallelujah!

A person may be heavy laden and needy, but emotional comfort and peace of mind are not sought. Seek the Lord and be gladdened by His presence. It is by praise and adoration that the thirsty soul finds he has been refreshed at the fountain of living water. If sad, the water has become like wine, the best wine to cheer the heart. A river flows. Enfolded in the Presence is like being in a refreshing pool of water, waters to swim in where stresses vanish, tensions are relieved, and troubles float away. "Better is one day in your courts than a thousand elsewhere" (Psalm 84:10a).

Clothed in a sumptuous robe of righteousness, enter the palace. God's child is brought to the banqueting hall. See Jesus. Seek His Face. Feast on His beauty, partake of His goodness and truth, and be satisfied with the richest of fare. The banner overhead is love.

Come into the throne room; the Lord is on His Heavenly Throne. God is holy, and this is a holy place, not the place to confess sins. A person is cleansed and made holy by the precious blood of Jesus. It is in the throne room that, by prayer and petition, with thanksgiving, requests are presented to God the Father. A child of God can pour out his heart to "Abba Father"—speak to Him about failures that trouble the heart and mind, of hurts and burdens. One can thank God for His blessings, talk of joys and plans, and make requests for needs, wants, and desires. Focus on Almighty God. To look at the problem instead of Him weakens one's faith. Nothing is too small for a loving God. Nothing is too big or complex for an all-powerful God.

A granddaughter was seriously ill and in the hospital. I was much impressed when her sister brought in a placard on which she had written "Don't tell God about your need, tell your need about your God." Trust the Lord. "Now to him who is able to do immeasurably more than all we ask or imagine, according to his power…to him be glory" (Ephesians 3:20).

Hearts break. Life hurts. Come into his presence. "The Lord is close to the broken hearted and saves those who are crushed in spirit" (Psalm 34:18). Life's desperate situations can wreak havoc on the physical body, the mind, and the emotions. The pain may be relentless and the trouble long term, but there is strength in prayer. Move in close to God. When devastated by trauma from sickness, disaster, death, or betrayal, the focus tends to be on the inner pain, but look to Jesus—seek Him.

At a time of ruinous sorrow, of mental and emotional turmoil, I asked God, "What am I going to do?" I clearly heard Him say, "Jesus." Feeling a little indignant I said, "I know, but I need an answer." Then I heard, "Jesus is the answer." Even in deep sorrow and loss, let the quest be for God, and there is an undergirding knowledge that all is well. "In the day of trouble he will keep you safe in his dwelling" (Psalm 27:5). His dwelling is His presence. In His presence, a peace that transcends understanding happens in the inner man and permeates the soul. God is near. Worship Him. Renewal and hope accompany worship. Man approaches God through his spirit by the Spirit, but what God does for man is done for the benefit and blessing of soul and body.

Intercession takes place in the Throne Room. God wondered and was appalled that there was no one to intervene, no one to intercede. Intercession is straightforward, but the seriousness of the transaction is seen in scripture. "Since my people are crushed, I am crushed; I mourn, and horror grips me" (Jeremiah 8:21). "Oh, that my head were a spring of water and my eyes a fountain of tears! I would weep day and night for…my people" (Jeremiah 9:1). "Let your tears flow like a river day and night; give yourself no relief, your eyes no rest. Arise, cry out in the night, as the watches of the night begin; pour out your hearts like water in the presence of the Lord. Lift up your hands to him for the lives of your children…" (Lamentations 2:18b-19).

Intercession is the result of a deep concern for loved ones, the lost among them, the sick, the needy, and the troubled. Intercede about a situation, circumstances, or a need. Indeed, intercede for a country's leaders to make laws fair and true that God's people have freedom to worship and serve Him. "…if we ask anything according to His will, He hears us. And if we know that He hears us—whatever we ask—we know that we have what we asked of Him" (1 John 5:14-15).

Celebrate God Almighty in His sanctuary. This is the celebration hall, a place of great exuberance. The heavens are stretched out like a canopy. Banners are flying. Pillars reach to the stars. "Your procession has come into view, O God, the procession of my God and King into the sanctuary" (Psalms 68:24). Hear the sounding of the trumpet heralding His presence. The Lord, high and lifted up, sits enthroned as King forever. Almighty God is celebrated in the sanctuary with pomp and circumstance. Worship Him with gladness. Come before Him with joyful songs. Exalt Him for His mighty power and Shekinah. "I have seen you in the sanctuary and beheld your power and your glory. Because your love is better than life, my lips will glorify you" (Psalm 63:2-3). Heavenly music, exquisite and sublime, stirs the senses, thrills the heart, and flows back to God in praise. God is praised with the dance of joy, the vibrancy and timbre of stringed instruments, the singular and clarion piping of the flute. Praise Him in His mighty heavens. The clash of resounding cymbals applauds Him for His acts of power and His surpassing greatness. "For this God is our God forever and ever" (Psalms 84:14a).

God! Majestic! Magnificent! Infinite!

Are there any whose heart-cry is "I want to know Him"?

About the Author

Claudia Lindsey was born in Browntown, Wisconsin, the daughter of a Methodist minister. Nearby Milwaukee became home until she left to attend Southwestern Bible College in Waxahachie, Texas. Here, she met her future husband who was there studying for the ministry. They were in active ministry for a number of years. In later life, Claudia managed a family-owned art gallery in New Bern, North Carolina. She and a son still reside in New Bern.

www.ingramcontent.com/pod-product-compliance
Lightning Source LLC
Chambersburg PA
CBHW071633040426
42452CB00009B/1602